Contents

CÈPE
Boletus edulis

MOREL
Morchella esculenta

CHANTERELLE
Cantharellus cibanus

FIELD MUSHROOM
Psalliota campestris

Introduction

The magic of mushroom cookery is fascinating to contemplate and the culinary realm of the fabulous fungi a delight to discover and explore. Of all our alluring foods, the mushroom is one of the most intriguing besides being wonderfully versatile and adaptable. By itself the mushroom is a gastronomic celebrity, but it also imparts richness and flavor to other foods. Mushrooms provide excitement, nourishment and savor to all elements of the culinary repertoire, either for everyday dining or special occasions.

Fortunately, mushrooms are in plentiful supply and of superb quality. This has not always been the case, for cultivated mushrooms, which Americans now consume by the millions of pounds each year, are a comparatively recent phenomenon. Wild mushrooms, a member of the fungi family which are believed to have been the first plants to appear on earth, have long attracted man with a strange and compelling fascination. Mysterious, marvelous, magical. Throughout the centuries these words have been applied to mushrooms in many lands. For centuries they were regarded with awe and superstition, associated with religions and believed to possess supernatural powers. The eating of some kinds is known to have induced colorful visions.

Seeing them appear almost magically overnight, the ancients believed that they were created by lightning bolts from the heavens. The Greeks called them *broma theon*, "food of the Gods." To the

Chinese they were treasured for medicinal properties as well as for food. The Pharaohs of Egypt cherished them as a special delicacy.

It is not impossible that the rulers of these long ago days subtly encouraged this air of mystery in order to reserve the sought-after food for themselves. Julius Caesar was more blunt. He flatly decreed the common man unworthy of the "treasures" and strictly limited their sale to the highborn and wealthy.

It was also known long ago that many of the numerous varieties of wild mushrooms were non-edible and that eating them would create grave illnesses or even death. Thus, many persons viewed the fantastic fungi with alarm rather than with gastronomic pleasure. But it is to the great credit of the mushroom that any unpleasant associations were sublimated by the food's enormous appeal at many a fine repast. Mushrooms over the years became very important to the cuisines of Russia, France, Germany and Italy, as well as to those of Japan and China. In Europe upperclass epicures developed an inordinate taste for the more delicate fungi species such as truffles, *cèpes* and *morels*, leaving ordinary mushrooms to become readily available for the common people and, when in season, a significant part of the daily diet.

A most important mushroom discovery occurred in the 17th century during the reign of Louis XIV while many minds were preoccupied with the improvement of fine fare. The French found out that mushrooms could be cultivated in caves and abandoned quarries and thus became the first to market the *Agaricus campestris*, the scientific name of the common field mushroom which is the only variety which can be grown commercially. Many of the "early" mushrooms came from the limestone caves of Paris and even today the small white ones grown throughout the *Ile de France* are still called *"champignons de Paris."*

In America, early colonists found mushrooms growing wild and learned to distinguish between the different varieties. The perils of eating them prevented many from appreciating the fine food, but some persons continued to do so and in 1895 Boston devotees of mushrooms formed a Mycological Club to promote further interest in a "neglected food" and to enjoy some savory dishes prepared with them. The cultivated mushroom, on the other hand, spread from France to England, and thence to America where, almost 90 years ago, Long Island residents began to grow them, primarily on the floors of cellars and caves. Florists in Chester County, Penn., also began growing them, under the benches of their green houses.

The greatest event concerning the growing of mushrooms in America occurred in 1926 when a farmer in Pennsylvania discovered a clump of pure white mushrooms in a bed of uniformly cream-colored caps. All of the millions of white mushrooms cultivated today are descendants of this small group, and since then the oyster-white plant has become better and better known on our tables. In fact, it is only on the West Coast and around the Chicago area that the light-tan or "brown" mushroom is preferred to the white one. The only difference between them is the color.

Large quantities of mushrooms are still grown in caves but the majority of them are raised on mushroom "farms" which have sprung up across the country. They are grown, for example, in California and the Pacific Northwest; regions around Chicago, St. Louis and Kansas City; and in Ohio, Southern Michigan, New York State and New England. The heart of the mushroom growing industry, however, is in Pennsylvania's Chester County where two-thirds of the cultivated crop is grown. Kennett Square, Penn., where the American Mushroom Institute is located, has been dubbed "the mushroom capital of the USA" and is visited by many interested persons who want to learn more about the lore of mushrooms.

Today the "food of the Gods" is produced in millions of pounds each year and is available daily in markets and stores at prices everyone can afford. A large part of the annual harvest is canned or used for soups, sauces and gravies. A few are dried. The rest are sold fresh in 7-ounce or 1-pound cartons, 3-pound baskets or in bulk. In most areas across the country mushrooms are generally available throughout the year, but they are at their best and most plentiful during the fall and winter.

Over the years man has learned a great deal about mushrooms and their eccentricities, but it still not easy to describe or define them.

According to Webster the mushroom is "any of the various rapid-growing, fleshy fungi having a stalk with an umbrellalike top." Besides the cultivated mushroom, the wild varieties number in the thousands and range in color from white to green, black or blue. The "umbrella" differs so greatly in shape that it may resemble a trumpet, cone or button and can be smooth, warted or spongy.

The mushroom is neither a root, fruit, herb or vegetable, even though as a food it is classified as a vegetable. Unlike other plants, it lacks chlorophyll, green coloring matter, and thus cannot manufacture its own food. It depends on other substances, living or dead, for its nourishment. Another distinction is that mushrooms do not have seeds. They are reproduced from spores of minute size and infinitesimal weight which drop from the undersides of mature mushrooms in such profusion that one "rain" can produce as many as one billion spores. Only one of these, however, will probably grow as a fruit of the plant, or mushroom.

The mushroom is very selective about its surroundings and will not grow unless the conditions are to its liking. Although large quantities of mushrooms are still grown in caves, the majority of them are carefully nurtured in specially designed mushroom houses under most exacting conditions of soil, moisture, humidity and temperature. Those houses with air conditioning can produce year-round crops. Since mushrooms prefer total darkness and require neither sunlight nor warmth, they are not permitted to see the light of day until hand-picked by workers who must wear miners' lamps in their caps to light their way. The fungi prefer to feed on decayed vegetable matter and must be given ample moisture while growing.

Once grown, the mushroom is picked at different stages and can have a cap as small as ¾ of an inch or as wide as 4 inches. Fresh young mushrooms or buttons, as the small ones are called, have closed caps since they are picked before they flatten out, and the gills or "veils" on the undersides do not show. Their stems are customarily short. Mature mushrooms have caps which have opened out to the typical umbrella shape exposing the gills. The stems tend to be a little longer than on the smaller ones.

The texture of the two kinds differs a little but not the flavor and for most cooks the size of a mushroom is of little consequence. One exception is perhaps the extra-large ones which are desirable to fill with special stuffings. Smaller buttons are slightly more delicate and thus regarded more highly. Since the ends of large stems are sometimes fibrous or woody and should be cut off, mushrooms with smaller stems are preferred. The flesh of the stem is nearly as soft as that of the cap but not as tender. The stems should not however be discarded. If only the caps are to be used, save the stems to make soups, sauces, gravies and stuffings. Or chop them, sauté and add to casseroles, egg dishes and stuffings. They are often used also as a filling, mixed with other ingredients, for the caps.

In purchasing mushrooms, it is important to choose dry and firm mushrooms without spots. The caps should be plump and of good shape with smooth skins. Buy mushrooms with mature or open caps only if they will be used shortly thereafter. Slight discolorations do not affect the flavor but indicate age. Another indication of age is the color of the gills, which start to darken as soon as the mushroom opens and begins to mature. Dark, wrinkled mushrooms should not be bought. Good fresh mushrooms can be refrigerated; place on a shallow rack or tray, cover with moistened paper toweling and store so air will circulate around them. They will keep a week or so. If they are frozen, unwashed, in sealed containers, they can be stored for as long as a month. Mushrooms sautéed until half done and frozen in containers will last for several months.

The basic preparation of mushrooms is very easy but not well understood by many cooks. Mushrooms, for example, should *never* be peeled. Much of their fine flavor and nutritional value is contained in the skins and should not be lost. To clean mushrooms it is usually only necessary to remove any dirt smudges by wiping quickly with a damp cloth or paper toweling. If it is necessary to wash them, rinse quickly under a stream of cold water and wipe dry at once. Mushrooms should *never* be soaked in water, for they behave very much like sponges and quickly absorb the liquid which is then suddenly released when they are heated. Thus the true flavor of the mushroom is lost. Prepare only as many at a time as you wish to cook.

Cultivated mushrooms can be served in any number of ways. They are delicious raw, sautéed, broiled, steamed or pickled, and they work magic in sauces, stuffings, stews, soups, omelets, fritters, salads and pastas, as well as with other vegetables, meats, poultry and seafood.

The familiar white or tan cultivated mushrooms are truly gastronomic treasures, but there are many mushroom lovers who regard the wild varieties, sometimes called "field mushrooms," with special reverence. In Europe wild mushrooms, whose flavor is more distinctive and stronger, are considered superior to the cultivated ones and are widely sought-after. Many a family enjoys a happy outing with a picnic and a mushroom-gathering "party", but only experts in distinguishing the various varieties should engage in picking them in fields. Those in markets are safe to purchase.

In America there are about 50 edible wild species, and although the sport of mushroom-hunting is not as common as in Europe, the enthusiasts are keen about it. They, at the first alert that the fungi have sprung up, dash with baskets and knives to that particular locale and will travel many miles to find a favorite variety.

Many of the best European and Oriental mushrooms are available in the United States at specialty or foreign grocery stores, either in cans or dried. Dried ones have a dark shriveled appearance and a very concentrated flavor. A few will go a long way and they are particularly recommended for stews, sauces and soups. Those that come from Europe are various shades of yellow or brown, whereas most of the dried mushrooms from the Orient are black. To prepare, they must be washed in cold water and then soaked in lukewarm water to cover in a non-metal container with a top for twenty to thirty minutes.

Three outstanding European wild mushrooms are quite well known to many Americans. In fact, one of them, the *morel*, grows also in the United States. It is generally considered to be finest of the fungi; it is very rare, with a short season and is most expensive to buy. The cone-shaped caps, indented with honey-combing, range in color from tan to dark brown. The *morel* must be washed very thoroughly to remove sand from its numerous indentations. Purists prefer *morels* sautéed in butter with perhaps a little cream, but they may also be prepared in several appealing ways similar to methods used for cultivated mushrooms.

Large, strongly-flavored French *cèpes*, ranging in color from yellow to reddish-brown, are highly esteemed in French cookery and are exported in cans or dried form. In America they sell for very fancy prices. Another excellent European mushroom is the *chanterelle* which is cup-shaped with a frilly edge and shallow gills and of a pale or dark egg yolk color. It is so distinctive that it cannot be confused with any other.

There is no foolproof way to distinguish between edible and nonedible mushrooms except by specific identification, so novices are warned and advised to leave the pleasure of hunting wild mushrooms to the experts. Fortunately, mushroom lovers can enjoy vast quantities of American cultivated mushrooms as well as wild fungi from many countries of the world in a fascinating variety of delectable dishes. The "food of the Gods" is now readily available for everyone.

Basic Data and Recipes

1. *Agaricus campestris*: the scientific name of the cultivated mushroom.

2. *Amanita*: poisonous mushrooms are members of this family. They are beautiful to behold, but eating them can result in serious illness or death.

3. *Availability*: cultivated mushrooms are generally available throughout the year. The peak season is from September to June. Fresh ones are sold in cartons, baskets and bulk. Canned ones are sold as caps, slices, stems and pieces, chopped or whole, with or without butter. Mushrooms are also available frozen, freeze-dried, and dried.

4. *Calories*: mushrooms are low in calories. One pound of raw mushrooms has 66 calories.

5. *Canned*: to enhance the flavor of canned mushrooms, drain, dry, and sauté in butter or oil for 3 to 4 minutes, depending on the size. Lemon juice may be added to the butter if desired.

6. *Cèpes*: large, strongly-flavored wild mushrooms, ranging in color from fawn to reddish-brown. Highly esteemed in French cookery. Available in the US in cans or dried form; expensive.

7. *Champignons de Paris*: the cultivated mushrooms sold in France. Creamy white in color.

8. *Chanterelles*: bright yellow, trumpet-shaped wild mushrooms with a delicate flavor. Imported from Europe in cans and dried form.

9. *Chinese*: dried, brownish and black mushrooms with caps averaging from ½″ to 2″ when dry but expand slightly when soaked. Excellent flavor. Available in Oriental and specialty food stores.

10. *Colors*: cultivated mushrooms sold in the US are pure white, except in California and Chicago where light-tan or brown ones are preferred. Wild mushrooms are of various colors.

11. *Cooking*: mushrooms require little cooking. Whole mushrooms cook in 4 to 5 minutes. Sliced, quartered or chopped, they require less time. In dishes requiring long cooking such as stews or casseroles, add raw mushrooms about 10 minutes before the dish is taken from the heat.

12. *Cultivation*: only one kind of mushroom, the *agaricus campestris*, is cultivated. Many attempts have been made to cultivate other varieties of mushrooms but none have been successful.

13. *Drying*: string firm fresh whole mushrooms through the center of the stem and on through the cap. Make knots in the string, separating mushrooms by one inch. Place on a large sheet of paper or hang in hot dry air for 2 or 3 days. Store in tightly covered jars.

14. *Equivalents for fresh and canned mushrooms*: 1 pound fresh = 1 eight-ounce can; ½ pound fresh = 1 four-ounce can; 20 to 24 fresh medium caps = 1 eight-ounce can; 1 quart fresh mushrooms = 1 eight-ounce can.

15. *Food value*: mushrooms have a relatively high phosphorous content as well as larger than average amounts of riboflavin, niacin and calcium pantothenate. They also contain other B vitamins, iron and copper. They have some protein and are low in sodium and fat.

16. *Freeze*: to freeze mushrooms, choose firm, fresh ones and place, unwashed, in freezer containers. Seal the tops. They will last one month. Mushrooms sautéed until half done, placed in freezer containers and sealed, will last several months.

17. *Frozen*: mushrooms which have been frozen can generally be used in the same manner as fresh ones. They taste more like fresh ones than canned mushrooms. Defrost and rinse quickly in cold water.

18. *Fungi*: a wide variety of plants that have no leaves, flowers or green color and reproduce by spores. Included in the family are mushrooms, molds and mildews.

19. *Kennett Square, Penn.*: "The mushroom capital of the US", and the site of the Mushroom Institute.

20. *Lemon Juice*: add fresh lemon juice to salted water when boiling mushrooms as it helps to keep them white. It is also added very often to sautéed mushrooms.

21. *Matsutake*: the renowned, fragrant delicate Japanese mushroom which is available in the US dried or canned.

22. *Morels*: the most delicate, tasty and sought-after of the wild mushrooms. Highly prized and expensive.

23. *Purchasing*: select firm, white mushrooms without spots. Fresh ones have closed caps and the gills cannot be seen. The stems are usually short. Mature or slightly aged mushrooms have caps opened to the typical umbrella-shape and the gills exposed. Buy the latter only if they will be used almost immediately.

24. *Raw mushrooms*: excellent in salads. The caps are tasty appetizers when stuffed. They may be served with dips such as a sour cream or an onion-flavored combination.

25. *Sauce*: mushroom sauce, a condiment made of soy sauce, spices, malt and vinegar, which can be served with meats and poultry

or used to flavor sauces, gravies, stews and baked dishes.

26.   *Seasonings*: excellent seasonings for mushrooms include: butter, olive oil, chives, shallots, nutmeg, ginger, paprika, marjoram, parsley, tarragon, rosemary and oregano.

27.   *Shiitake*: Japanese "tree mushroom" which for a very long time, has been cultivated in water-soaked logs. Available in the US dried.

28.   *Size*: the size of a mushroom is no indication of its quality or flavor. Larger caps are desired by cooks to be stuffed or used as garnishes.

29.   *Spores*: the "seeds" of mushrooms which fall from the undersides of mature mushroom caps in great quantity.

30.   *Stems*: mushroom stems are not quite as tender as the caps. Mushrooms with shorter stems are of better quality as the longer ones are sometimes woody or tough. Cut off any of these portions and discard. Use stems for soups, sauces, and stews, or chop, sauté and use with other dishes. To remove stems from the caps, gently pull off.

31.   *Storage*: place fresh mushrooms on a shallow tray and cover with a dry paper towel moistened with water and wrung half dry. Place on refrigerator shelf where air will circulate around them. If the paper toweling is moistened each day, mushrooms will keep fresh for several days.

32.   *Water*: mushrooms do not mix well with water since they absorb it too quickly and, when heated, rapidly release the liquid along with much of the mushroom flavor.

33.   *Wild*: there are thousands of wild mushrooms, including both edible and non-edible varieties. In the US there are about 50 edible varieties. Since there is no way to distinguish definitely between them except by specific identification, only mushroom experts should "hunt" them.

Basic Recipes

Sautéed Mushrooms

It is very important to sauté mushrooms correctly in order to enhance their flavor and maintain high quality. Sautéed mushrooms may be added to other dishes, served as an accompaniment to steaks and roasts, or served as a luncheon or supper dish. The mushrooms should be dry, the oil or butter hot, and the mushrooms not crowded together while cooking. If there are too many mushrooms, they will be steamed instead of sautéed. Some cooks prefer a combination of butter and oil, others, plain butter or oil. Mushrooms shrink and lose their juices if not sautéed properly.

Heat a large heavy skillet or griddle. Add enough butter or oil, or butter and oil, to coat the surface generously. Keep adding as needed. When very hot and browned, but not burned, place dry mushrooms, whole or sliced, over the surface, in one layer and not touching. Test for heat. They should begin to sizzle at once. Watch carefully. When the edges begin to brown and the centers are clear, turn each one over. Lightly brown on the other side. The cooking takes about 4 minutes. Lift out onto paper toweling. Dust lightly with salt and, on occasion, a little ground ginger. Sprinkle with lemon juice if desired, just before serving.

(Note: canned mushrooms require a little less cooking time than fresh ones.)

To sauté caps: brown first on the round side. The time will be a little longer than for sliced mushrooms, perhaps 6 to 8 minutes, depending on the size of the caps.

Variations:

> *Provençale*: add minced onion, crushed garlic, chopped tomatoes and fresh herbs.
>
> *à la Russe*: add a little paprika and sour cream.
>
> *Italiano*: add minced green onions, tomato paste, minced garlic, and herbs such as basil, oregano or parsley.
>
> *English*: add a little thick cream and chopped herbs.
> *à la Bordelaise*: add chopped shallots, garlic and a mixture of herbs (chives, chervil, parsley, tarragon).

Mushroom Butter

1 cup minced raw mushrooms   *2 teaspoons lemon juice*
¼ pound butter   *Salt, pepper to taste*

Combine the ingredients. Use as a spread for canapes or sandwishes or spread over broiled mushrooms, steaks or chops. Add 1 crushed small garlic clove, if desired.

Broiled Mushrooms

Broiled mushrooms are an excellent garnish when served with steaks, or they may be served as an appetizer on toast. They are also good on hamburgers or grilled tomatoes or served as a separate vegetable. The mushrooms should be fresh and of the best quality. Many cooks prefer the large flat caps for broiling but smaller ones may also be used.

Clean the mushrooms. Pull off the stems. Rub the caps inside and out with butter or oil. Place, round sides up, in a shallow baking dish. Put under a broiler, about 5 inches below the heat, and cook 4 minutes. Turn over the caps and broil another 4 to 5 minutes. Remove from the heat and add to each cap ¼ teaspoon butter, salt, freshly ground pepper and a little lemon juice. Just before serving, return to broiler and let the butter sizzle inside the mushrooms.

Variations:

1. Combine chopped herbs with butter.

2. Spoon chopped garlic and chopped shallots or green onions into the caps.

3. Italians add a little oregano or marjoram and garlic to the butter.

4. When cooked, sprinkle with dry sherry.

Baked Mushroom Caps

Wash and dry the fresh mushrooms. Pull off the stems and cut off any tough stem ends. Chop the stems. Sauté the caps in oil or butter. Remove with a slotted spoon to a buttered shallow baking dish. Sauté the chopped stems in the drippings; spoon into the caps. Sprinkle with lemon juice, salt and pepper. Bake in a preheated moderate oven (350 F.) for 25 to 30 minutes.

Variations:

1. Sprinkle with white wine and chopped parsley.

2. Add fine dry bread crumbs and minced onions to the stems. Sprinkle with oil before baking.

3. Add chopped garlic, tomatoes and oregano to the stems.

4. Add grated nutmeg and cream to the stems.

Creamed Mushrooms

½ pound fresh mushrooms
2 tablespoons butter
1 tablespoon salad oil
2 tablespoons minced shallots
  or green onions

Salt, pepper to taste
1 tablespoon flour
1 cup heavy cream

Wash and dry the mushrooms. Chop or slice. Sauté in the hot butter and oil for 3 minutes. Add the shallots and sauté 1 minute. Season with salt and pepper. Stir in the flour; blend well. Add the cream and cook slowly, stirring, until heated and well blended. Serve on toast, on small rounds of bread or in tart shells.

Mushroom Aspic

1½ pounds fresh mushrooms
½ cup chicken stock
Juice of ½ lemon
Salt, pepper, nutmeg to taste

1 envelope plain gelatine
½ cup cold water
1 tablespoon dry sherry

Clean the mushrooms. Cut off any tough stem ends. Chop or slice. Cook in the stock with the lemon juice, salt, pepper and nutmeg over moderate heat about 6 minutes. Dissolve the gelatine in the water and stir into the hot mixture. Add the sherry and remove from the heat. Pour into a mold or a small bowl. Chill until set. Unmold. Chop or cut into any desired shapes and use as a garnish. Or serve on salad greens garnished with sour cream.

Duxelles

Duxelles, a sautéed preparation of seasoned chopped mushrooms, is named after the 17th century French gourmet, Marquis d'Uxelles, whose famous chef, LaVarenne, is credited with its creation. The classic mixture can be kept on hand in the refrigerator or freezer to use in a number of interesting ways. It is an excellent filling for mushroom caps, fish or vegetables, or, mixed with bread crumbs, for poultry. *Duxelles* may be mixed with eggs to make an omelet, or added to sauces. It is an excellent spread for canapes or sandwiches.

1 pound fresh mushrooms	3 tablespoons minced onions
1/4 cup butter	1 garlic clove, crushed
2 tablespoons salad oil	Salt, pepper to taste
3 tablespoons minced shallots or green onions	1 tablespoon chopped fresh parsley

Clean the mushrooms. Cut off any tough stem ends. Chop mushrooms very finely. Press in a cloth to remove any moisture. Heat the butter and oil over a hot fire. Add the shallots, onions, and garlic and sauté 1 minute, stirring constantly. Lower the heat and add the minced mushrooms. Sauté until all the moisture has evaporated and the mixture is quite dark. This may take quite a long time. Season with salt and pepper. Stir in the parsley. Makes 2 cups.

Appetizers, Hors d' Oeuvre

The magic of mushrooms can be readily appreciated when used as appetizers and hors d'oeuvre, whether a selection for a few persons or an elaborate array for hundreds. Either raw or cooked, they are tempting to the eye, tasteful to the palate and stimulating to the appetite.

In gastronomic nomenclature appetizers are customarily regarded as appealing foods to be enjoyed with beverages before a meal or at a party. They are usually dainty and easy to handle. Hors d'oeuvres, on the other hand, also delight the eye but are usually a little more substantial and are sometimes served with a fork. Many of them may also be served as a first course.

Cold and hot culinary delights made with mushrooms have long been popular at before-the-meal gatherings around the world. Early Greeks enjoyed them with goblets of wine as "provocatives to drinking." In Russia the elaborate display of *zakuski* features mushrooms, pickled, stuffed and mixed with other vegetables or sour cream. For a Scandinavian *Smorgasbord* they are used in souffles, puddings, omelets and fish dishes. In Central Europe they are most popular when seasoned piquantly. The French hors d'oeuvre and Italian antipasto show off the fungi in salads or mixed with fresh herbs. In the Orient, native tid-bits often include mushrooms seasoned with traditional sauces.

However or wherever they are served, some of the classic mushroom dishes from other nations are a particular delight to prepare and taste. They also combine well with many American favorites to offer the hostess an excellent repertoire. On any occasion, whether an informal family get-together or an elaborate event for many friends, the following recipes will provide an intriguing variety of appetizers and hors d'oeuvre.

Russian Mushroom Caviar

In Russia there are two appetizers, one made with eggplant and the other with mushrooms, which have been dubbed poor man's or peasant's caviar. Presumably they are eaten as substitutes for the expensive black pearls of sturgeon caviar. The mushroom caviar, however, is excellent fare and especially good with black bread or pumpernickel. Offer in a bowl surrounded with pieces of bread.

1 cup chopped onions
⅓ cup butter or margarine
1 teaspoon paprika
2 cups chopped raw
    mushrooms
2 tablespoons wine vinegar

Salt, pepper to taste
⅓ cup chopped fresh dill or
    parsley
⅔ cup sour cream
2 tablespoons chopped chives
    or green onions

Sauté the onions in the butter until tender. Stir in the paprika and cook 1 minute. Add the mushrooms, vinegar, salt and pepper; sauté 4 minutes. Stir in the dill and sour cream and leave over a low fire long enough to heat through. Serve garnished with the chives. Serves 4.

Continental Beignets de Champignons

European hostesses very often serve one excellent hot, light appetizer with apéritifs before a special dinner. These fritters are perfect for such an occasion.

1 cup flour	¾ cup sautéed chopped
1½ teaspoons baking powder	mushrooms
½ teaspoon salt	2 teaspoons minced green
2 eggs, separated	onions
⅓ cup milk	Fat for frying
Freshly grated nutmeg	

Sift the flour, baking powder and salt into a bowl. Combine the egg yolks and milk and add to the dry ingredients. Stir in the nutmeg and beat well. Whip the egg whites until stiff. Fold them, the mushrooms and onions into the flour mixture. Drop by teaspoonsfuls into hot deep fat (375°F. on a frying thermometer) until golden brown. Drain on absorbent paper. Makes about 25 small fritters. Serve warm, with sour cream if desired.

Austrian Egg and Tomato "Mushrooms"

In Austria, and Germany as well, mushrooms have long been symbols of good luck. Replicas of white-stemmed mushrooms with red and white speckled caps, made of wood, glass, china or earthenware, are sold as Christmas tree ornaments, home decorations, candle holders and other various things. An edible replica that appears frequently on the appetizer table is made with hard-cooked eggs and tomatoes. It may be used as a garnish or served as an hors d'oeuvre.

4 *shelled hard-cooked eggs*   *Mayonnaise*
2 *medium-small tomatoes—*
   cut in half crosswise

Cut a slice from the end of a hard-cooked egg so it will stand upright. Remove the pulp, seeds and liquid from the tomato halves. Fit each over an egg to form a "cap." Decorate the tomato top with tiny specks of mayonnaise. Serves 2 as an hors d'oeuvre.

Provençale Pan Bagna

In the lovely sun-kissed area of Provence in southern France a favorite picnic food is a marvelous filled round loaf of crusty bread. The ingredients are generally those native to the locale, such as green peppers, olives, onions, tomatoes and anchovies. They vary, however, with each preparation. This is one suggestion.

Slice 1 round or 1 long loaf of crusty French bread in half lengthwise. Sprinkle the surface of one side with olive oil and rub with garlic. Arrange slices of fresh mushrooms, tomatoes, sweet onions, hard-cooked eggs and radishes over it. Top with drained flat anchovy fillets, halved pitted black olives and pieces of green pepper. Sprinkle lightly with vinegar. Top with the other bread half. Press together and slice. Serves 6.

Mushroom Kebabs

An appealing way of serving mushroom caps is to arrange them alternately with other attractive ingredients on small wooden skewers. The possibilities are numerous. These are but two suggestions.

I.

24 medium, fresh mushrooms	¾ cup olive or salad oil
2 packages (9 ounces each) frozen artichoke hearts, cooked & drained	1 teaspoon mustard seeds ⅓ cup chopped fresh parsley Salt, pepper, cayenne to taste
1 cup wine vinegar	Cherry tomatoes

Clean the mushrooms. Remove the stems. Place the caps and cooked artichoke hearts in a bowl. Cover with the remaining ingredients, except the tomatoes, and marinate 3-4 hours. Drain. Place on small wooden skewers alternately with the tomatoes. Broil 3 inches from the heat, about 4 minutes, turning once. Serve at once. Serves 4 to 6.

II.

24 cleaned, shelled cooked medium shrimps	24 pitted ripe olives White wine
24 cleaned raw mushroom caps	Dried basil Salt, pepper, paprika to taste

Place the shrimps, mushrooms and olives in a bowl. Sprinkle generously with white wine, basil, salt, pepper and paprika. Marinate 3-4 hours. Drain. String alternately on skewers and serve. Serves 4 to 6.

Spanish Sausage and Mushrooms

Arrange 1 Spanish sausage, *chorizo*, sliced (or another highly-spiced pork sausage) on a plate. Surround with 10 sautéed, large mushroom caps, gill sides up, and sprinkled with chopped fresh herbs and onions. Serves 2.

Mushrooms Italiano

For an easy-to-prepare antipasto, serve this flavorful dish with black and green olives, slices of salami, chunks of tuna, radishes and caper-garnished hard-cooked egg wedges.

½ pound fresh mushrooms
2 large tomatoes, peeled &
    chopped
½ cup minced green pepper

2 tablespoons fresh lemon
    juice
⅓ cup chili sauce
½ teaspoon dried oregano
Salt, pepper to taste

Clean the mushrooms. Pull off the stems and use for another dish. Slice the caps thickly. Combine with the other ingredients and leave to marinate at room temperature 2 to 3 hours. Serve as an antipasto or with crusty bread as an appetizer. Serves 2.

Hungarian Mushroom-filled Eggs

6 hard-cooked eggs, shelled
½ cup finely chopped mush-
    rooms, fresh or canned
2 tablespoons butter or
    margarine
1 teaspoon paprika

Salt, pepper to taste
½ teaspoon dry mustard
3 tablespoons (about) sour
    cream
Chopped chives or green
    onions

Cut the eggs in half lengthwise. Remove the yolks and mash. Sauté the mushrooms in butter for 3 minutes. Add the paprika and sauté 1 minute. Season with salt and pepper. Add the mashed egg yolks, mustard and enough sour cream to bind the mushroom mixture. Spoon into the egg shells, shaping the mixture into a mound on each egg half. Garnish with the chives. Serves 6. Serve as an hors d'oeuvre or on lettuce leaves as a first course.

Mushrooms on Toast from Germany

The Germans enjoy mushrooms in a number of inviting ways as ingredients for their appetizers, *vorspeisen*. This variation of *champignon-schnitt* may also be served as a first course or luncheon dish.

1 pound fresh mushrooms	*Salt, freshly ground pepper,*
½ cup butter	*grated nutmeg to taste*
Juice of 1 lemon	*8 toasted firm white bread*
¼ cup flour	*slices, crusts removed*
1½ cups rich brown gravy	*Chopped fresh parsley*
½ cup dry white wine	

Clean the mushrooms and wipe dry. Slice. Heat the butter and lemon juice in a skillet. Add the mushroom slices and sauté for 2 minutes. Stir in the flour and half the gravy. Cook, stirring, 1 minute. Stir in the remaining gravy, wine, salt, pepper and nutmeg. Cook, stirring, about 2 minutes. Cut the toast into triangles and spoon the hot mushroom mixture over them. Sprinkle with parsley. Serves 4 to 6.

Pickled Mushrooms, Japanese Style

An unusual appetizer which may be prepared beforehand and kept ready in the refrigerator.

1 pound small fresh	*3 tablespoons vinegar*
mushrooms	*1-2 tablespoons soy sauce*
4 green onions with tops,	*1 tablespoon sugar*
minced	*Pepper to taste*
3 tablespoons mirin* *or dry*	
sherry	

Clean the mushrooms. Remove the stems. Cook the caps in boiling salted water to cover for 5 minutes. Drain and cool. Cover with the remaining ingredients and leave at room temperature for 24 hours. Serve on small wooden skewers. Serves 8 to 10.

**Mirin* is sold at Oriental or specialty food stores.

Champignons à la Grecque

The French have given us the culinary description "à la Grecque" which generally refers to cooked vegetables prepared with oil, vinegar or lemon juice and seasonings, and served cold. Mushrooms are great favorites for this type of preparation. When marinated in this way, they are excellent for impromptu entertaining as they can be kept for several days in the refrigerator.

1 pound small fresh	*2 garlic cloves, crushed*
mushrooms	*1 bay leaf*
4 tablespoons lemon juice	*¼ teaspoon dried oregano*
Salt to taste	*3 sprigs parsley*
½ cup olive oil	*4 peppercorns*

Clean the mushrooms. Pull off the stems and reserve for another use. Cook the caps in salted boiling water to cover with 1 tablespoon lemon juice for 5 minutes. Drain and cool. Bring the remaining ingredients to a boil. Put the cooled mushroom caps in a jar. Cover with the boiled marinade. Leave, shaking now and then, 2 to 3 days in the refrigerator. Drain. Serve on toothpicks or small wooden skewers. Serves 8 to 10.

Mushroom and Crabmeat Canapés

1 cup cooked diced
    mushrooms
1 cup cooked flaked crabmeat
3-4 tablespoons mayonnaise
6 drops onion juice
¼ cup grated Parmesan
    cheese

Cayenne, salt, pepper to taste
18 small rounds lightly
    toasted white bread
Butter
Mustard

Combine the mushrooms, crabmeat, mayonnaise, onion juice, Parmesan, cayenne, salt and pepper; mix well. Spread each round of bread with butter and mustard. Top with some of the crabmeat mixture. Serve cold or heat in a hot oven (400° F.) about 10 minutes. Serves 6 to 8.

Persian Mushroom-Borani

A most appealing appetizer is the Persian *borani*, a flavorful combination of yogurt and a vegetable. The Persians, or Iranians, as they are now known, eat it with bread as a first course. It may be also served as a substitute for salad or an accompaniment to meat or poultry.

1 large onion, finely chopped
3 tablespoons butter or
    margarine
2 tablespoons lemon juice
1 pound fresh mushrooms,
    cleaned & sliced

Salt, pepper to taste
1 cup plain yogurt
3 tablespoons chopped fresh
    mint

Sauté the onion in the butter until tender. Add the lemon juice and mushrooms and sauté 4 minutes. Season with salt and pepper. Stir in the yogurt and chopped mint. Chill. Serves 4.

Mushroom-Artichoke Cocktail

An excellent first course for a company luncheon or dinner.

1 pound small fresh
    mushrooms
2 tablespoons lemon juice
2 packages (9 ounces each)
    frozen artichoke hearts
1/3 cup wine vinegar
1/2 cup olive oil

2 garlic cloves, crushed
1/4 teaspoon dried thyme
1/4 teaspoon dried chervil
Salt, pepper to taste
Chopped chives or green
    onions

Clean the mushrooms. Pull off the stems and use for another dish. Boil the caps with the lemon juice in salted water to cover for 5 minutes. Drain and cool. Cook the artichokes according to package directions. Drain and cut into halves. Cool. Combine with the mushrooms in a bowl. Cover with the vinegar, oil, garlic, thyme, chervil, salt and pepper. Leave at room temperature for 1 hour mixing about now and then. Serve in individual dishes garnished with chopped chives. Serves 6.

Mexican Tacos filled with Mushrooms

In Mexico the typical appetizers, *antojitos,* literally "little whims", are sold at street stands, sidewalk cafes and just about every restaurant so they can be enjoyed any hour of the day. One of the best is the *tacos* which make an excellent appetizer when filled with these inviting ingredients.

1 pound sliced fresh mushrooms	2 large tomatoes, peeled & chopped
1 medium onion, chopped	Chili powder, salt, pepper to taste
2 canned green chilis, chopped	Tomato sauce (optional)
1 cup shredded lettuce	12 tortillas
	Hot shortening (lard or oil)

Combine the mushrooms, onion, chilis, lettuce, tomatoes, chili powder, salt and pepper and toss lightly. Moisten a little with tomato sauce, if desired.

Dip the tortillas into the hot shortening long enough to become limp. Remove with tongs and fold over. Spoon filling over each and fold over like a small sandwich. Serves 12.

Miniature Mushroom Pizzas

Since the end of World War II one of America's most popular foods inside and outside of the home has been an import from Naples, the pizza. This is an excellent impromptu version to serve teenagers with soft drinks or adults with other beverages.

Toast 4 English muffins, cut in half. Sprinkle each with a

little olive oil and rub with garlic. Top with a slice of mozzarella cheese and a layer of sliced mushrooms. Top with a
spoonful of tomato sauce. Bake in a preheated hot oven (400° F.)
for 10 minutes, or until the cheese is melted. Serves 4.

Lithuanian Herring-Mushroom Appetizer

Like other Eastern Europeans, the Lithuanians are extremely
fond of several basic and nourishing foods which they combine
to make interesting dishes. Three of them, herring, mushrooms
and sour cream, are included in this dish.

2 medium onions, sliced	Freshly grated pepper
3 tablespoons shortening (lard	4 pickled herring, sliced
or other shortening)	2 tablespoons chopped fresh
2 cups sliced mushrooms,	dill or parsley
canned or fresh	

Sauté the onions in the shortening until soft. Add the mushrooms and sauté 4 minutes. Season with pepper. Cool. Mix with
the herring and serve cold garnished with the dill. Serve with
sour cream, if desired. Serves 4.

Mushroom Appetizers Orientale

2 cups sliced mushrooms,	2 cups canned bean sprouts,
fresh or canned	drained
3-4 tablespoons soy sauce	2 teaspoons sugar
1 garlic clove, crushed	1/4 cup minced green onions,
4 tablespoons sesame or salad	with tops
oil	2 tablespoons dry sherry

Place the mushrooms in a bowl and cover with the soy sauce, garlic and 2 tablespoons sesame oil. Rinse the bean sprouts in cold water. Sauté them in the remaining 2 tablespoons of oil for 5 minutes. Add the mushrooms and their marinade and sauté 4 minutes. Stir in the sugar, green onions and sherry. Serve warm in small dishes. Makes 6 servings.

Russian Mushroom-filled Piroshki

Among the many delectable foods in the Russian array of appetizers (*zakuski*) are the small filled pastries called *piroshki*. They are made with short pastry or yeast dough and stuffed with mixtures of beef, fish or vegetables, particularly mushrooms. The Russians also enjoy them when served with bowls of soup, such as borsch, for a first course.

1 envelope active dry yeast or 1 cake yeast	½ pound fresh mushrooms
1 cup lukewarm milk	3 tablespoons butter
2 teaspoons sugar	1 large onion, minced
Salt	Pepper to taste
½ cup butter or margarine, melted	3 tablespoons chopped fresh dill or parsley
3 eggs, slightly beaten	⅓ cup sour cream
5 cups sifted flour	1 egg yolk, well beaten

Put the yeast in a large warmed bowl. Add 2 tablespoons of the lukewarm milk and stir to dissolve the yeast. Combine the sugar, 1 teaspoon salt, melted butter and eggs with the remaining milk. Stir in the dissolved yeast. Add the flour, a little at a time, stirring well after each addition. Turn out on a floured board and knead until smooth and elastic. Shape into a large ball and put in a buttered bowl; turn over. Let rise, covered, in a warm

(80°F.) place for 1½ hours or until double in bulk.

Meanwhile, clean the mushrooms. Cut off any woody stems. Chop finely. Melt the butter in a skillet and add the onions. Sauté 2 minutes. Add the mushrooms, salt and pepper and sauté 4 minutes. Stir in the dill and sour cream. Remove from the heat and cool.

Punch down the dough. Turn out on a floured board and knead. Pinch off small pieces of dough and flatten into thin 3 inch circles. Place 2-3 teaspoons of filling in the center of each. Bring up the dough around the filling to secure completely and shape into a smooth round. Place on a greased cookie sheet. Let rise for 20 minutes in a warm place. Brush with beaten egg yolk. Bake in a preheated hot (400°F.) oven about 20 minutes, until golden and flaky. Makes about 35 *piroshki*. Serve warm.

Mushroom-Clam Dip

Typical American appetizer creations which are very popular for cocktail parties are creamy mixtures called dips which are scooped up with a variety of foods, such as crackers and raw vegetables. This is an interesting variation which is sure to attract attention at any festive get-together.

2 cups chopped raw mushrooms	1 teaspoon prepared horseradish
2 tablespoons lemon juice	2 cans (10½ ounces each) minced clams, drained
3 tablespoons chopped chives	
Dash or two of Tabasco	2 cups sour cream
	Paprika

Combine all the ingredients except the paprika and chill for several hours. Serve, garnished with paprika, in a bowl surrounded by raw vegetables, including whole mushrooms if desired, or crackers. Makes about 5 cups.

English Mushroom Beef Tartare

In England, and other European countries as well, a very popular appetizer is beef tartare, raw ground beef combined with raw egg yolks and seasonings. The name is believed to have derived from the Tartar practice of scraping and eating raw meat. Purists maintain that the best meat for the appetizer is obtained by scraping lean beef. Ground beef, however, is excellent but should be freshly ground at least twice.

1½ cups chopped mushrooms, fresh or canned
3 tablespoons butter
2 tablespoons lemon juice
Salt, freshly ground pepper to taste
1½ pounds lean round or sirloin steak, ground twice
2 egg yolks, slightly beaten
2 garlic cloves, crushed
⅓ cup finely chopped onion
2 teaspoons dry mustard
1-2 teaspoons Worcestershire sauce
½ cup chopped fresh parsley

Sauté the mushrooms in the butter with the lemon juice for 4 minutes. Season with salt and pepper. Combine with the meat, egg yolks, garlic, onion, mustard and Worcestershire in a large bowl and mix well. To serve, pat smooth into a mound or loaf on a wooden board or tray. Garnish with the parsley. Surround with thin slices of rye bread and pumpernickel. Makes 12 to 15 servings.

NOTE: This elegant appetizer may also include capers and anchovy fillets and can also be served in canape form on small rounds of dark or white bread.

Polish Mushrooms Smetana

For an intimate gathering of four persons, serve this appealing appetizer on individual small plates. In Poland it would be enjoyed with vodka.

1 medium onion, chopped	2 tablespoons milk
3 tablespoons butter	Salt, pepper to taste
2 teaspoons paprika	1 cup sour cream
1 pound thickly sliced fresh mushrooms	Rye bread slices
2 tablespoons flour	Chopped fresh dill

Sauté the onion in the butter until soft. Stir in the paprika and cook 1 minute. Add the mushrooms and sauté 4 minutes. Stir in the flour and blend well. Add the milk, salt and pepper and cook, stirring, until thickened. Stir in the sour cream. Serve warm, spooned onto squares of rye bread and sprinkled with chopped dill. Makes 4 servings.

Mushroom-Herb Appetizer

1 pound fresh mushrooms	1 cup chopped fresh herbs
3 tablespoons butter	(watercress, tarragon,
2 tablespoons lemon juice	chervil, parsley)
Freshly grated nutmeg	Garnishes: tomato wedges,
Salt, pepper to taste	cucumber slices, black olives

Clean the mushrooms. Cut off any woody stem ends. Slice

thickly from the round sides through the stems. Sauté in the butter and lemon juice for 4 minutes. Season with nutmeg, salt and pepper. Mix in the herbs and serve at once with the garnishes. Makes 4 servings.

Mediterranean Cold Vegetable Hors d'Oeuvre

In the lovely warm Mediterranean countries a lengthy luncheon is very often preceded by an assortment of colorful and well-seasoned hors d'oeuvre, each served in a separate small dish. This typical dish may be served alone with chunks of crusty bread or accompanied by such foods as olives, cucumber slices, wedges of cheese, radishes, and anchovy fillets or sardines.

1 cup sliced onions
2 garlic cloves, crushed
⅓ cup olive or salad oil
2 large tomatoes, peeled &
    chopped
1 cup sliced fresh mushrooms

2 tablespoons lemon juice
1 package (9 ounces) frozen
    French cut green beans
Salt, pepper to taste
¼ cup chopped fresh parsley

Sauté the onions and garlic in the heated oil in a saucepan until tender. Add the tomatoes and sauté until mushy. Mix in the mushrooms and lemon juice and sauté 3 minutes. Add the green beans, salt and pepper. Cook slowly, about 15 minutes, until the beans are tender. Stir in the parsley and remove from the heat. Serve cold. Makes 4 to 6 servings.

Salade de Champignons

In France many of their appealing salads are served as hors d'oeuvre in small glass dishes, *raviers*, which are set on a side table or cart so that diners can choose from an inviting assortment. Mushrooms are customarily included in many of these salads. The preparations are quite simple.

One way is to mix thinly sliced fresh mushrooms with good French dressing and garnish with chopped chives or green onions and perhaps also chopped fresh herbs.

Another easy-to-prepare salad is made by sprinkling sliced fresh mushrooms with lemon juice, olive oil, dried thyme, chopped parsley, salt and pepper.

Raw Mushroom Open-Faced Sandwich

1 cup sliced raw mushrooms
3 tablespoons French dressing
1 tablespoon catsup

¼ to ½ teaspoon prepared
    horseradish
Salt, pepper, cayenne to taste
2 slices dark toast

Combine the ingredients, except the toast, and marinate at room temperature for 30 minutes. Spread over the toast. Garnish with minced chives or green onions, if desired. Cut each slice into 2 triangles. Serve on individual plates with forks. Serves 2.

Stuffed Mushrooms

Of the many mushroom creations, some of the most popular are those prepared by stuffing the caps with various fillings. The caps may be raw, boiled, baked or broiled and eaten both hot and cold. Some fillings are simple such as cheese and butter; others may be complicated preparations such as sherried lobster. They may be served as appetizers, first courses, luncheon or supper entrées or accompaniments to meats or poultry. Generally, small or medium sized caps are served as appetizers and the larger ones for other courses.

The caps, if cooked, are usually boiled or sautéed before stuffing. Once filled, they are either baked or broiled. Stuffed mushrooms may be prepared beforehand and frozen, arranged in layers in freezer containers or on aluminum plates. Defrost and reheat in a moderate oven for several minutes, the exact time depending on the size.

Given below are two recipes and several suggestions for stuffings.

Baked Italian Mushrooms

1 pound large fresh mushrooms	½ cup chopped fresh parsley
1 cup dry breadcrumbs	Salt, pepper to taste
1-2 garlic cloves, crushed	Olive oil
3 tablespoons grated Parmesan cheese	Small rounds of white toast

Clean the mushrooms. Pull off the stems and use for another dish. Sauté the caps in heated olive oil for 4 minutes. Drain and arrange, gill sides up, in a buttered shallow baking dish. Stir the breadcrumbs into the olive oil drippings, adding more oil if necessary, and sauté until well coated with the oil. Mix in the garlic, grated cheese, parsley, salt and pepper. Remove from the heat and spoon into the mushroom caps. Sprinkle with oil. Bake in a preheated moderate oven (350°F.) for 15 minutes. Spoon onto the small rounds of toast. Serves 4 to 6.

Some suggested fillings include:
1. Cooked sausage meat, steak sauce, minced green onions and curry powder.

2. Blue cheese, butter and sherry.
3. Smoked oysters, lemon juice and chopped parsley.
4. Finely chopped ham, breadcrumbs, chopped stems and grated Parmesan cheese.
5. Liver pâté, cream, sherry and chopped chives.
6. Minced cooked sole, chopped stems, nutmeg, and thick cream.
7. Minced onions, chopped parsley, cooked ground beef and dry red wine.
8. Chopped stems, cream cheese and paprika.
9. Cooked crabmeat, mayonnaise and chopped dill.
10. Chopped cooked bacon, chopped onion, crushed garlic, tomato paste and basil.

Champignons Farcis

1 pound extra-large fresh
    mushrooms
¼ cup minced green onions
Butter
⅓ cup minced cooked seafood

Salt, pepper, fresh ground
    nutmeg to taste
1 tablespoon chopped fresh
    parsley

Clean and dry the mushrooms. Remove the stems and mince. Sauté the onion in ¼ cup of the butter until tender. Add the minced stems and sauté for 4 minutes. Add the remaining ingredients. Mix well and cool. Brush the caps generously with melted butter and arrange in a shallow dish. Place in a preheated moderate oven (350°F.) until tender, 15-20 minutes. Fill the caps with the seafood mixture, sprinkling the top with a little melted butter. Brown in the oven and serve with forks. Serves 4 to 6.

Soups

In the realm of soups, there is a galaxy of tempting creations from which to choose for everyday or company meals. Since the beginning of time man has combined a variety of available ingredients into appealing soups to provide daily sustenance or to enhance a regal repast. Each country has several favorite basic soups which are robust, nourishing and filling, as well as more aristocratic combinations which are lighter and designed to stimulate the appetite.

Mushrooms have long been important to the making of both varieties of soup and many a classic recipe includes them. In Europe, for example, they are considered essential for several of the favorite household soups which are carefully made with only the finest of ingredients. An excellent basic stock is prepared with the marvelous dried mushrooms. Russians dote on barley-mushroom soup. Italians flavor a delectable one with Marsala. The Poles are devoted to the addition of sour cream to mushroom broth, and the French repertoire includes numerous appealing variations.

The best known soup in the galaxy, cream of mushroom, is so readily available in America in cans that many people might wonder about preparing it themselves. The canned soup is excellent for making sauces, casseroles and combining with other foods, but with no disrespect to the manufacturers, that made in the home can be even better.

Old-fashioned methods of preparing soups involved a great deal of work and hours of cooking broths and stocks. The cook today is fortunate in having ready-made consommés, bouillon cubes and broths which are wonderful for preparing soups without a great deal of trouble. Mushrooms add additional flavor and sparkle to the long-time favorites as well as to newer creations. For instance, chowders, beloved by our grandparents, are given added flavor by the addition of mushrooms. When sliced and sautéed, they add zest to a blender-made *potage* of frozen broccoli and light cream.

In selecting a soup, its purpose should be considered. For a supper or prelude to a light meal, a hearty kind is the proper choice. As a first course the lighter varieties should be served. The rest of the menu should also be considered. With a spicy entrée, serve a bland first-course soup and vice versa. Cream soups do not harmonize with main courses that include cream sauces.

Soup should be served as attractively as possible and may be offered in a variety of ways, such as in small or large bowls, cups or glasses, or it can be ladled from a large tureen. A befitting accolade to soup in the latter container was offered by Alice in Wonderland who cried:

> "Beautiful soup, so rich and green
> Waiting in a hot tureen!
> Who for such dainties would not stoop?
> Soup of the evening, beautiful soup."

Chicken Mushroom Pot from Hungary

A good one-dish meal seasoned with that great Hungarian favorite, paprika. Some cooks also add sour cream to the soup just before serving it.

1 stewing chicken, about 4 pounds, washed & cut-up	1 celery root, pared & cut up
3 quarts water	¾ pound whole small fresh mushrooms

1 bouquet garni (*parsley sprigs, thyme, bay leaf*)
Salt, pepper to taste
1 *parsnip, pared & cut up*
2 *carrots, scraped & sliced*

1 *pound fine egg noodles, cooked & drained*
2 *tablespoons butter*
2 *teaspoons paprika*

Put the cut-up chicken in a large kettle with the water, *bouquet garni*, salt and pepper. Bring to a boil and skim. Reduce the heat and cook slowly, covered, for 1½ to 2 hours. Take the chicken pieces from the broth and cut off the meat, discarding the skin and bones. Cut the chicken into bite-size pieces and return to the broth. Add the parsnip, carrots and celery root and cook slowly, covered, for 30 minutes or until the vegetables are tender. Add the mushrooms during the last 5 minutes of cooking. Stir in the noodles, butter and paprika. Makes 8 to 10 hearty servings.

Curried Avocado-Mushroom Soup

Native to Central and South America, the avocado once grew wild. Today it is widely cultivated in our country, particularly in California and Florida although it did not become widely available until a few years ago. Today, like mushrooms, avocados are standard items in our supermarkets. These two delicate foods combine to make a different and inviting rich soup.

1 *cup sliced fresh or canned mushrooms*
2 *tablespoons butter or margarine*
1 *tablespoon lemon juice*

Salt, pepper to taste
1 *large or 2 small avocados*
3 *cups chicken broth*
2 *level teaspoons curry powder*
1 *cup light cream or milk*

Sauté the mushrooms in the butter and lemon juice for 2 minutes. Season with salt and pepper and set aside. Cut the avocado in half; remove seed and skin. Whirl until smooth in a blender or put through a sieve. Add 1 cup of chicken broth and the curry powder and blend again. Combine with the remaining broth in a saucepan and heat gently . Add the cream and sautéed mushrooms, with the drippings, and leave on the stove long enough to heat through. Season with salt and pepper. Serves 4.

Israeli Mushroom Herb Soup

The Israelis are very particular about their fare and have many important rules governing their diet, both for everyday and religious holiday meals. There is a list of forbidden foods, but it does not include such good fare as mushrooms and herbs which they combine to make a flavorful soup.

1 cup chopped onions
⅓ cup butter or margarine
2 tablespoons fresh lemon juice
2 cups sliced mushrooms, fresh or canned

4 cups strained vegetable stock or 4 vegetable bouillon cubes and 4 cups of water
¾ cup chopped mixed fresh herbs (basil, chervil, tarragon or water cress)
Salt, pepper to taste

Sauté the onions in the butter in a saucepan until tender. Add the lemon juice and mushrooms and sauté 4 minutes. Pour in the vegetable stock. Add the herbs, salt and pepper. Cook over medium heat, covered, for 30 minutes. Serves 4 to 6.

Soupe a l'Oignon aux Champignons

An interesting version of that traditional French favorite, onion soup, which is good at any hour of the day or night.

⅓ cup butter

4 cups sliced onions

6 cups beef bouillon

½ pound sliced fresh mushrooms
    or 1 can (8 ounces) sliced
    canned mushrooms, drained

Salt, pepper to taste

Toasted slices of French bread

Grated Parmesan cheese

Melt the butter in a large saucepan. Add the onions and cook over low heat until tender. Do not brown. Add the bouillon and bring to a boil. Mix in the mushrooms, salt and pepper. Lower the heat and cook slowly, covered, for 30 minutes. Pour into bowls. Top with the toast. Sprinkle with grated cheese. Serves 4 to 6.

Southern Corn-Mushroom Soup

An easy-to-prepare soup for a light family meal. Serve with hot corn bread.

1 cup sliced fresh mushrooms
    or 1 can (about 4 ounces)
    sliced mushrooms, drained

5 tablespoons butter

1 tablespoon lemon juice

½ cup chopped onion

3 tablespoons flour

3 cups milk

¼ teaspoon cayenne

Salt, pepper to taste

1 can (1 pound) cream-style
    corn

⅓ cup minced green pepper

Sauté the mushrooms in 2 tablespoons of the butter and lemon juice for 4 minutes if fresh, 3 if canned. Set aside. Melt the remaining 3 tablespoons of butter in a saucepan. Add the onions and sauté until tender. Stir in the flour to blend well. Gradually add the milk, stirring as added, and cook until smooth and thick. Season with cayenne, salt and pepper. Mix in the corn, sautéed mushrooms and green pepper and leave on the stove long enough to heat through. Serves 6.

Zuppa di Funghi Italiana

For a party, serve teen-agers this soup with pizzas.

1 pound fresh mushrooms	½ teaspoon dried basil
3 tablespoons butter	Salt, pepper to taste
3 tablespoons finely chopped onion	1 cup broken spaghetti, cooked & drained
1 large garlic clove, crushed	2 tablespoons chopped fresh parsley
¼ cup tomato purée	Freshly grated Parmesan
1 quart beef or chicken bouillon	

Rinse the mushrooms quickly, or clean with wet paper toweling to remove any dirt. Slice lengthwise through the caps. Melt the butter in a large saucepan. Add the onion and garlic and sauté until soft. Add the mushrooms and sauté 2 minutes. Pour in the tomato purée and bouillon. Add the basil, salt and pepper. Bring to a boil. Lower the heat and cook slowly, covered, for 30 minutes. Add the spaghetti and parsley and cook 1 minute. Serve with grated Parmesan. Serves 6.

Viennese Beef Soup with Rice and Mushrooms

Austrians are partial to a wide number of good soups but their indisputable favorite is that called *Rindsuppe* which is made with beef. There are many versions but each is prepared with top quality meat and the best of vegetables. This substantial soup may be served as a supper dish.

1 large onion, chopped
1 large carrot, diced
1 large stalk celery, diced
2 leeks, white parts only,
    sliced
2 large fresh or canned
    tomatoes, peeled &
    chopped
3 tablespoons butter

2 pounds soup beef, meat and
    bones
2 quarts water
2 whole cloves
1/4 teaspoon dried thyme
3 sprigs parsley
Salt, pepper to taste
1/3 cup uncooked rice
1/2 pound fresh mushrooms,
    thickly sliced

In a large kettle combine the onion, carrot, celery, leeks, tomatoes and butter. Sauté the vegetables for 5 minutes. Push aside and add the soup meat and bones. Brown on all sides. Add the water, cloves, thyme, parsley, salt and pepper and bring to a boil. Lower the heat and cook slowly, covered, for 1 hour. Add the rice and continue to cook for another 30 minutes. Mix in the mushrooms 10 minutes before the cooking is finished. Take out the meat and bones. Cut the meat into small pieces, removing and discarding any fat or gristle. Return to the soup. Remove and discard the cloves. Serves 8 to 10.

Spinach Mushroom Soup Orientale

This soup is typical of those made with mushrooms in the Orient. It is nutritious and appealing to the palate and the eye.

2 tablespoons sliced green
    onions, with tops
1 tablespoon peanut oil
1/2 cup sliced bamboo shoots
6 cups chicken broth

1/2 pound fresh spinach,
    cleaned & chopped
1/4 pound fresh mushrooms,
    thinly sliced
4 ounces fine egg noodles
Salt, pepper to taste

Sauté the onions in the oil in a large saucepan. Add the bamboo shoots and broth and bring to a boil. Stir in the spinach and mushrooms and cook, covered, over medium heat for 10 minutes. Add the egg noodles and cook, uncovered, about 7 minutes. Season with salt and pepper. Serves 6 to 8.

Chilled Mushroom Madrilène

A good summer dish.

2 cans (12½ ounces each)
   madrilène soup
1 pound small fresh
   mushrooms

⅓ cup fresh lemon juice
1 tablespoon chopped chives
Salt, pepper to taste

Chill the madrilène. Clean the mushrooms and slice from the round sides through the stem ends. Mix with the lemon juice, chives, salt and pepper and leave 30 minutes. Turn out the chilled madrilène into a large bowl. With a fork, break up. Combine with the mushroom mixture and chill again until ready to serve. Serves 6.

Swiss Mushroom Consommé

A refreshing soup to serve as the first course of a hearty meal.

¾ pound fresh mushrooms
3 tablespoons butter
8 cups beef consommé
Freshly grated nutmeg

1 cup dry sherry
2 tablespoons minced green
   onions, with tops, or
   chopped fresh parsley

Salt, freshly ground pepper to
taste

Rinse the mushrooms quickly or wipe them with wet paper toweling to remove any dirt. Sauté in the butter in a large saucepan for 2 minutes. Add the consommé, nutmeg, salt and pepper. Cook, covered, over moderate heat for 10 minutes. Add the sherry and green onions and leave on the stove just long enough to heat through. Serves 8.

Chinese Black Mushroom Soup

One of the most notable of all the many mushrooms is the large black variety from China. They have exceptional flavor. Fortunately we can purchase them dried in Oriental stores and they are well worth seeking.

12 medium-size dried black
*   mushrooms*
2 quarts beef bouillon
½ cup minced green onions

½ cup bamboo shoots
4 water chestnuts, sliced
2-3 tablespoons soy sauce
Pepper to taste

Soak the mushrooms in lukewarm water to cover for 20 minutes. Drain, retaining the liquid. Slice thickly. Heat the beef bouillon to boiling. Add the mushrooms with the liquid, green onions, bamboo shoots and water chestnuts. Lower the heat and simmer, covered, for 30 minutes. Add the soy sauce, the amount according to taste, and the pepper. Remove from the heat. Serves 8.

Mushroom-Tomato Soup

Serve with grilled Swiss cheese sandwiches for a winter supper.

1 *pound fresh mushrooms*	1 *quart tomato juice*
4 *green onions with tops,*	½ *teaspoon dried basil*
minced	*Salt, pepper to taste*
3 *tablespoons butter*	1½ *cups light cream or milk*
2 *tablespoons flour*	

Clean the mushrooms. Cut off any tough stem ends. Slice from the round sides through the stems. Sauté the onions in the butter in a saucepan until tender. Add the mushroom slices and sauté 4 minutes. Stir in the flour; blend well. Add the tomato juice, basil, salt and pepper. Simmer, covered, for 10 minutes. Add the cream and leave on the stove long enough to heat through. Serves 4 to 6.

Scandinavian Fisksoppa with Mushrooms

Scandinavians are extremely fond of the wide range of fungi readily available in their northern lands. Children are taught at an early age how to identify each of wild varieties which are picked at family outings with great glee. Unfortunately, Americans do not have all of these kinds available, but a good Scandinavian soup can be made with cultivated mushrooms.

2 *leeks, white parts only,*	½ *teaspoon nutmeg*
sliced	*Salt, pepper to taste*

½ cup sliced onions
1 stalk celery, sliced
3 medium potatoes, diced
⅓ cup butter or margarine
1½ quarts water
2 whole cloves

1 pound white fish fillets
  (halibut, cod, haddock)
  cut into bite-size pieces
1 can or jar (about 4 ounces)
  sliced mushrooms, drained
2 teaspoons chopped fresh dill

Sauté the leeks, onions, celery and potatoes in the butter until the onions are soft. Add the water, cloves, nutmeg, salt and pepper and cook 5 minutes. Add the fish fillets and cook until they are just tender, about 12 minutes, and the potatoes are cooked. Add the mushrooms 5 minutes before the cooking is finished. Serve garnished with the dill. Remove and discard the cloves. Serves 6 to 8.

Mushroom Clam Bisque

Rich and creamy bisques have long been favorite fare for elegant dinners. They have also been highly praised in literature. Writers have complimented a bisque as being "the most royal of royal dishes," "a food for princes and financiers," and "the object of divine worship." Such a noteworthy specialty should properly be served at a handsomely set table with pretty appointments.

½ pound fresh or 1 can
  (4 ounces) sliced
  mushrooms
4 tablespoons butter or
  margarine
2 tablespoons lemon juice
½ cup finely chopped onion
2 tablespoons flour

2 bottles (8 ounces each)
  clam juice
2 cans (7 ounces) minced
  clams
3 cups light cream
½ teaspoon celery salt
Salt, pepper to taste
2 tablespoons chopped parsley

Sauté the mushrooms in 2 tablespoons of butter and the lemon juice for 4 minutes, if fresh, and 3 if canned. Set aside. Heat the remaining 2 tablespoons of butter in a saucepan and stir in the onions. Sauté until tender. Mix in the flour to blend well. Gradually add the clam juice, stirring as added until thick and smooth. Add the clams, cream, celery salt, salt and pepper and sautéed mushrooms with the drippings. Leave on the stove long enough to heat through. Serve garnished with the parsley. Serves 6.

Polish Barley-Mushroom Soup

Barley, one of the world's oldest cereal grasses and earliest cultivated grains, has long been cherished for its nutty flavor and high nutrition. It has been a particularly important food in the cuisines of Scotland, Scandinavia and Central Europe where there are a number of excellent barley soups. In Poland barley has given its name to this popular soup, *krupnik*.

3 ounces dried mushrooms	½ cup pearl barley
1 medium onion, chopped	2 quarts beef bouillon
1 leek, white part only, chopped	Salt, pepper to taste
1 celery stalk, chopped	½ cup sour cream, at room temperature
3 tablespoons butter	Chopped fresh dill or parsley

Soak the mushrooms in lukewarm water to cover for 20 minutes. Drain, pressing to extract any water. Slice the mushrooms. Sauté the onion, leek and celery in the butter in a large saucepan until the onion is tender. Add the barley and sauté 1 minute. Pour in the bouillon. Add the salt and pepper and bring to a boil. Lower the heat and simmer, covered, for 1 hour. Add the mushrooms and continue to cook about 30 minutes or until the barley is tender Stir in the sour cream and leave on the stove long enough to heat through. Serve garnished with dill. Serves 8.

Sherried Mushroom Lobster Bisque

An excellent luncheon dish.

¾ pound fresh mushrooms
¼ cup minced onion
6 tablespoons butter
3 tablespoons flour
5 chicken bouillon cubes
5 cups boiling water
⅛ teaspoon marjoram

Salt and pepper
1 tablespoon lemon juice
1½ cups cooked lobster,
cubed
1½ cups light cream
½ cup Sherry

Wash the mushrooms quickly or wipe with wet paper toweling to remove any dirt. Remove stems from the caps. Set aside caps; chop stems, discarding any tough ends. Sauté the onion in 3 tablespoons of butter in a large saucepan. Add flour; mix well. Add the chopped mushroom stems, bouillon cubes, boiling water, marjoram, salt and pepper. Simmer, covered, 25 minutes. Strain the mixture, pressing the mushrooms to release their juices.

Meanwhile, slice the mushroom caps and sauté in the remaining 3 tablespoons of butter and lemon juice for 3 minutes. Add, with the lobster and cream, to the strained liquid. Heat over a low fire; do not boil. Mix in the sherry just before serving. Serves 8 to 10.

Russian Potato Soup with Mushrooms

In Russia, housewives keep strings of dried mushrooms hanging in the kitchen so they are readily available for the many dishes prepared with them. They also use fresh ones in season.

1 large onion, chopped
1 large carrot, diced
1 leek, white part only, chopped
5 tablespoons butter or margarine
6 cups water
2 sprigs parsley
1 bay leaf

Salt, pepper to taste
2 pounds (about 6 medium) potatoes, peeled & cut up
1 cup chopped fresh mushrooms
1 tablespoon lemon juice
1 cup sour cream, at room temperature
2 teaspoons chopped fresh dill

Combine the onion, carrot, leek and 3 tablespoons of butter in a kettle. Sauté the vegetables for 5 minutes. Add the water, parsley, bay leaf, salt and pepper and bring to a boil. Lower the heat and cook slowly, covered, for 30 minutes. Add the potatoes and continue cooking about 20 minutes, or until the potatoes are just tender. Meanwhile, sauté the mushrooms in the remaining 2 tablespoons of butter and the lemon juice for 3 minutes. Stir, with the sour cream, into the soup. Leave on the stove just long enough to heat through. Serve garnished with the dill. Serves 6 to 8.

Rumanian Sauerkraut Tchorba with Mushrooms

The Rumanians are fond of soups with sour tastes, often achieved with fermented juices or sour fruits. This one, combining sauerkraut and sour cream, is characteristic of this typical flavor.

3 ounces dried mushrooms
1 cup lukewarm water

2 cups drained sauerkraut
6 cups beef bouillon

1 large onion, chopped
1 large carrot, diced
3 tablespoons butter or
    margarine
1 can (1 pound, 3 ounces)
    tomatoes

½ teaspoon dried thyme
1 bay leaf
Salt, pepper to taste
1 tablespoon vinegar
1 cup sour cream at room
    temperature

Soak the mushrooms in the water for 20 minutes. Drain, pressing to extract all the water. Reserve the liquid. Slice the mushrooms and set aside. Sauté the onion and carrot in the butter for 5 minutes. Add the tomatoes, sauerkraut, bouillon, thyme, bay leaf, salt and pepper. Bring to a boil. Lower the heat and simmer, covered, for 30 minutes. Stir in reserved mushroom liquid and mushrooms and continue to cook for 30 minutes longer. Remove from the heat. Take out and discard the bay leaf. Stir in the vinegar and sour cream while still hot. Serves 8 to 10.

Old World Ham-Pea Potage with Mushrooms

Save this recipe for the occasion when you're wondering what to do with a left-over ham bone. Dried mushrooms impart a particularly desirable flavor to the combination of ham and green peas, but canned or fresh mushrooms may be used as a substitute. For supper, serve with cheese pumpernickel sandwiches.

1 medium onion, chopped
1 large carrot, diced
1 large celery stalk, chopped
3 tablespoons oil or fat
1 baked ham bone
2 quarts water

1 pound split green peas
1 bay leaf
2 sprigs parsley
Salt, pepper to taste
3 ounces dried mushrooms

Sauté the onion, carrot and celery in the oil in a kettle for 5 minutes. Add the remaining ingredients, except the mushrooms. Bring to a boil. Lower the heat and cook slowly, covered, for about 1½ hours. While cooking, soak the mushrooms in lukewarm water to cover for 20 minutes. Drain, pressing to extract any water and discard the liquid. Slice the mushrooms and add to the soup 15 minutes before it is finished. Remove the ham bone. Cut any meat from it and chop. Return to the soup. Discard the bone. Take out and discard the bay leaf. Serves 6.

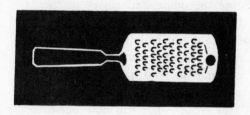

New England Seafood Chowder with Mushrooms

Over the years New England cooks have devised a number of hearty soups combining their rich bounty of seafood and vegetables. The name for this favorite fare, however, came from France where a *chaudière* is a short-legged kettle. Prepare this chowder in any large utensil and serve with hot corn bread or whole-grain bread for an inviting winter evening repast.

2 *ounces salt pork, diced, or*
  2 *slices bacon, chopped*
	1 *cup canned salmon,*
	  cleaned & flaked

⅓ *cup sliced onions*	3 *cups light cream or milk*
2 *cups diced raw potatoes*	1 *can* (4 *ounces*) *mushroom*
½ *cup water*	*stems and pieces, drained*
Salt, pepper to taste	2 *tablespoons chopped fresh*
½ *pound white fish fillets,* *cut-up*	*parsley*

Put the pork or bacon in a heavy kettle and fry. Add the onions and sauté until soft. Stir in the potatoes. Add the water, salt and pepper. Cook, covered, over medium heat for 5 minutes. Add the fish pieces and continue cooking until the fish is tender and the potatoes are tender, about 10 minutes. Add the salmon, cream and mushrooms and leave on the stove long enough to heat through. Serve garnished with the parsley. Serves 6.

Czech Fresh Mushroom Soup

In Czechoslovakia both the Czechs and Slovaks are hearty eaters who cherish their national dishes. For such hard-working folk soups are important fare and a beginning for most meals. Typical seasonings are those used here: caraway seeds, sour cream and dill. They combine with the flavor of mushrooms to make an interesting first course.

½ pound fresh mushrooms	Salt, pepper to taste
3 tablespoons butter	1 egg yolk
¼ teaspoon caraway seeds	1 cup sour cream, at room
4 green onions, with tops, sliced	temperature
1 tablespoon flour	1 tablespoon chopped fresh dill or parsley
4 cups beef bouillon	

Clean the mushrooms by rinsing quickly or wiping with wet paper toweling. Slice thickly. Sauté in the butter in a kettle with the caraway seeds and onions for 2 minutes. Mix in the flour to blend well. Gradually add the bouillon, stirring as it is added. Simmer, covered, for 30 minutes. Whip the egg yolk with a fork until creamy. Mix with the sour cream and dill. Spoon some of the hot soup to mix with it. Return to the soup and leave over low heat, stirring, 1 or 2 minutes. Serves 6.

Chilled Yogurt-Mushroom Potage

To surprise and delight guests, serve this refreshing cold soup for a summer meal. It may be offered in glasses or cups to guests before they are seated at the table or served in bowls as a first course. In the Middle East, where yogurt is a staple food, cold soups are very often garnished with sprigs of mint.

2 cups chopped mushrooms, fresh or canned	3 tablespoons butter or margarine
½ cup minced green onions, with tops	2 tablespoons fresh lemon juice
1 garlic clove, crushed (optional)	¼ teaspoon ground nutmeg
	Salt, white pepper to taste
	6 cups plain yogurt

Sauté the mushrooms, green onions and garlic in the butter and lemon juice in a kettle for 3 minutes. Add the nutmeg, salt and pepper. Remove from the heat and cool. Combine with the yogurt and chill. Serves 6 to 8.

Mushroom Minestroni

So important and varied is minestrone in Italy that each family has its favorite recipe. It is said to have been originated in olden days by monks who kept large pots of the soup for

wayfarers. Thus came the name, from the Latin for "hand out."
Mushrooms add further appeal to the hearty dish which is excellent supper fare. Serve with warm crusty bread.

1/4 cup minced salt pork or
    bacon
1 tablespoon olive oil
1 medium onion, chopped
1 garlic clove, crushed
1 large carrot, diced
2 large fresh or canned
    tomatoes, peeled & cut up
1 zucchini, sliced
1 cup chopped cabbage

6 cups water or bouillon
1 teaspoon dried basil
Salt, pepper to taste
1 cup cooked dried white
    beans
1 cup elbow macaroni
1/2 pound whole medium,
    fresh mushrooms, cleaned
Grated Parmesan cheese

Heat the pork and oil in a large kettle. Add the onion and
garlic and sauté until soft. Add the carrot, tomatoes, zucchini
and cabbage and cook for 5 minutes. Add the water or bouillon,
basil, salt and pepper and bring to a boil. Lower the heat and
cook slowly, covered, for 30 minutes. Add the beans and macaroni and cook until the macaroni is tender. Stir in the mushrooms
10 minutes before the cooking is finished. Serve with grated
Parmesan. Serves 8 to 10.

Korean Mushroom Soup

In Korea soup, *kook,* is served at most meals, including
breakfast, and is kept hot in small brass bowls. A great number
of the soups are made with vegetables, such as cabbage, spinach,
green onions, cucumbers and the ever-popular mushrooms, both
fresh and dried. Each soup is seasoned with the traditional
favorites of garlic, green onions, sesame seeds and pepper. This is
a typical light soup, excellent as a first course.

½ pound lean beef	3-4 tablespoons soy sauce
1 garlic clove, crushed	Pepper to taste
3 green onions, minced, with tops	2 tablespoons peanut oil
2 teaspoons toasted sesame seeds*	6 cups water
	1 cup sliced fresh mushrooms

onions, sesame seeds, soy sauce and pepper. Heat the oil in a large saucepan and add the beef mixture. Brown on all sides. Add the water and mushrooms and cook 30 minutes. Serves 4 to 6.

*Fry the seeds in a skillet over medium heat until brown. Remove and cool.

Potage Crème de Champignons

The French have several excellent recipes for making their favorite cream of mushroom soup, some richer than others. This one is a compromise selection, not too difficult to prepare but delightful to eat, perhaps for luncheon.

1 pound fresh mushrooms	3 tablespoons minced onions
5 tablespoons butter	2 tablespoons flour
1 tablespoon fresh lemon juice	6 cups chicken broth
Salt, white pepper to taste	1 bay leaf
2 tablespoons minced shallots or green onions	2 parsley sprigs
	Dash cayenne
	¾ cup heavy cream

Wash the mushrooms quickly or wipe them with wet paper

toweling to remove any dirt. Pull the stems from the caps. Cut any tough ends from the stems and chop finely. Slice the caps. Melt 2 tablespoons of butter in a large saucepan. Add the sliced caps and lemon juice and sauté 3 minutes. Season with salt and pepper. Remove to a plate.

Melt the remaining 3 tablespoons of butter in the saucepan. Add the shallots and onions and sauté until soft. Add the chopped mushroom stems and sauté 2 minutes. Stir in the flour and cook over low heat, stirring constantly, for 1 to 2 minutes. Gradually add the chicken broth, stirring as adding. Add the bay leaf, parsley, cayenne, salt and pepper. Cook over very low heat, mixing often, for 15 minutes. Strain, pressing the mushrooms with a spoon to release all the juices. Return the strained liquid to the saucepan. Add the sautéed sliced mushrooms and drippings and the cream. Leave on the stove long enough to heat through. Correct the seasoning. Serves 4 to 6.

Italian Mushroom Soup with Marsala

A good soup for the first course of a company dinner.

½ pound fresh mushrooms	2 tablespoons tomato paste
3 tablespoons butter	Salt, pepper, nutmeg to taste
1 garlic clove, crushed	½ cup Marsala wine
4 cups chicken broth	3 cups light cream or milk

Clean the mushrooms and cut off any tough stem ends. Cut into thick slices. Melt the butter in a saucepan and sauté the mushroom slices with the garlic for 2 minutes. Add the chicken broth, tomato paste, salt, pepper and nutmeg and simmer 15 minutes. Stir in the Marsala and cream and leave on the stove long enough to heat through. Serves 6 to 8.

Circassian Vegetable-Yogurt Soup with Mushrooms

The beautiful Circassian ladies who were brought from Southern Russia to the Sultans' courts at Constantinople in yester-year were noted for their culinary talents. A number of dishes found in the Middle East can be credited to them. The flavor of this vegetable and yogurt combination is enhanced by another Russian favorite, mushrooms.

1 beef soup bone
Salt, pepper to taste
1 bay leaf
1½ quarts water
1 large onion, chopped
⅓ cup uncooked rice
1 cup each of diced carrots,
  green beans and peas

2 cups tomato juice
½ teaspoon dried thyme
1 teaspoon paprika
½ pound fresh mushrooms,
  thickly sliced
1 cup plain yogurt

Put the soup bone, salt, pepper, bay leaf and water in a large heavy kettle. Bring to a boil and skim. Lower the heat and cook slowly, covered, for 1½ hours. Skim again. Add the onions, rice, vegetables, tomato juice, thyme and paprika. Continue to cook slowly, covered, for about 30 minutes, or until the meat, rice and vegetables are tender. Add the mushrooms 5 minutes before the soup is cooked. Remove the soup bone and discard. Add the yogurt and leave on the heat long enough to warm through. Do not boil. Serves 10 to 12.

Two recipes for easy-to-prepare soups using condensed Cream of Mushroom Soup follow.

Chilled Asparagus-Mushroom Soup

1 can (10 ounces) condensed
    cream-of-asparagus soup
1 can (10 ounces) condensed
    cream-of-mushroom soup
2 soup cans milk

⅓ cup dry sherry
Salt, pepper, freshly grated
    nutmeg to taste
2 tablespoons chopped chives

Combine the soups, milk, sherry, salt, pepper and nutmeg in a saucepan. Mix well and heat. Cook slowly 10 minutes to blend flavors. Cool and chill several hours. Serve garnished with the chives. Serves 4 to 6.

Curried Mushroom Soup with Chicken

2 cans (10 ounces each)
    condensed cream-of-
    mushroom soup
2 soup cans milk
1 cup diced, cooked chicken

2 tablespoons curry powder
½ teaspoon paprika
1 teaspoon Worcestershire
    sauce
Salt, pepper to taste

Combine all the ingredients in a saucepan and heat through over a low fire. Serve garnished with paprika. Serves 4 to 6.

Egg, Cheese and Luncheon Dishes

Two of our most important and versatile foods, eggs and cheese, marry most agreeably with mushrooms. Culinary creations made with eggs and mushrooms, cheese and mushrooms, or all three, are generally light and easy to prepare. They are superb for luncheon main dishes, and many are also excellent for company brunches, breakfast buffets, suppers and late evening parties.

Man has been enjoying a fascinating repertoire of fine fare made with eggs and cheese since he first domesticated poultry and animals and was thus assured of everyday supplies of eggs and milk.

Cheese is the world's oldest man-made food. Its creation, however, was probably accidental. One legend credits an ancient traveller in the desert with its discovery. When stopping for a meal, he poured milk from a pouch made of a sheep's stomach and found that the liquid had separated into curds and whey. The rennet of the stomach had done the trick. The unknown wanderer presumably found the curds, or cheese, both tasty and refreshing and told others about it.

Cheese was eaten in the Bible lands during ancient times. The early Greeks trained their Olympic heroes on cheese, thinking it possessed divine powers. The Romans developed the technique of cheese-making and introduced the art to the rest of Europe. Early colonists in America made cheese they had known in their homelands. Today we have a vast selection, both domestic and imported, to eat and to use in cooking.

The egg has long been an important part of our everyday dining. It is nutritious and plays many gastronomic roles. Since ancient times the egg has also been used as an important symbol, particularly to signify new life. Thus, it has been a treasured food for religious meals and is often served at holiday repasts.

Over the years, inventive cooks have found that the magic of mushrooms will transform basic egg and cheese dishes into elegant creations. Soufflés, omelets, *quiches*, pancakes, puddings, baked dishes, pies and sandwiches can become fascinating and festive fare for exceptional family and company meals.

Soufflé de Champignons

From the French we have inherited a number of excellent soufflé dishes. The word is taken from the French for "puffed up", and each soufflé is a glorious inflated creation which must be served directly from the oven, as it quickly deflates. This one may be served as a first course or as a luncheon entrée.

4 *eggs*	1 *cup finely chopped mush-*
1 *additional egg white*	*rooms, fresh or canned*
1 *tablespoon minced shallots*	*Dash freshly grated nutmeg*
or green onions	*Salt, pepper to taste*
4 *tablespoons butter*	3 *tablespoons flour*
1 *tablespoon lemon juice*	1 *cup milk*

Before starting to make the soufflé, remove the eggs from the refrigerator to bring to room temperature. Separate, putting the yolks in a small bowl and the whites with the additional white in a larger bowl.

Sauté the shallots in 1 tablespoon of butter with the lemon juice until soft. Add the mushrooms and sauté about 3 minutes. Season with nutmeg, salt and pepper and remove from the heat.

In a saucepan, melt the remaining 3 tablespoons of butter. Stir in the flour to form a *roux*. Cook, stirring, 1 minute. Gradually add the milk, stirring constantly, and cook slowly until thick and smooth. Remove from the heat and cool a little. Beat the egg yolks until creamy and mix into the white sauce. Stir in the mushroom mixture. Beat the egg whites until stiff. Carefully fold half of them into the mushroom combination. Then add the remaining half. Spoon the mixture into a buttered 1½ quart soufflé dish or casserole. Bake, uncovered, in a preheated moderate oven (375°F.) about 30 to 35 minutes, until puffed up and golden. Serve at once. Serves 4.

Sicilian Eggs with Vegetables

In the Mediterranean countries favorite dishes are made by combining eggs with flavorful sun-kissed vegetables, particularly such treasured items as eggplant and tomatoes. This is typical of such popular fare.

1 small eggplant, washed	½ cup white wine
Olive or salad oil for frying	½ teaspoon dried basil
1 large onion, chopped	Salt, pepper to taste
1-2 garlic cloves, crushed	2 tablespoons chopped fresh
½ pound whole small fresh	parsley
mushrooms, cleaned	8 eggs
1 can (1 pound) Italian style	2 tablespoons grated
tomatoes	Parmesan cheese

Cut the unpeeled eggplant into cubes. Put in a colander and sprinkle with salt. Leave for 30 minutes. Drain and wipe dry. Fry in heated oil in a large skillet until soft. Remove with a slotted spoon and set aside. Add more oil to the skillet, if needed. Add the onion and garlic and sauté until soft. Add the mushrooms and sauté about 3 minutes. Mix in the tomatoes. Add the wine, basil, salt and pepper. Return the eggplant to the skillet. Cook slowly, covered, for 15 minutes. Add the parsley and mix well. With the back of a large spoon make 8 depressions in the vegetable mixture. Break an egg into each depression. Sprinkle with the cheese. Cook slowly, covered, until the eggs are set. Serves 4 as a luncheon dish.

Chinese Mushroom Foo Yong

There are many versions of the Chinese omelet which is called *foo yong*. This one has the added flavor of mushrooms.

2 *tablespoons soy sauce*
1½ *tablespoons cornstarch*
1 *cup bouillon or cold water*
1 *teaspoon sugar*
¼ *cup minced green onions*
3 *tablespoons peanut oil*
¼ *cup diced ham*

½ *cup chopped mushrooms, fresh or canned*
¼ *cup diced celery or bamboo shoots*
¼ *cup chopped water chestnuts*
6 *eggs*
Salt, pepper to taste

In a small saucepan, heat the soy sauce. Dissolve the cornstarch in the bouillon or cold water and add, with the sugar, to the soy sauce. Mix well and heat, stirring, until thickened. Keep warm while preparing the *foo yong*.

Sauté the onions in the oil in a large skillet. Add the ham, mushrooms, celery and water chestnuts and sauté, stirring, for 1 minute. Spoon into a bowl. Beat the eggs slightly. Season with salt and pepper. Add to the mushroom mixture. Pour into a well greased skillet and cook, tilting the pan occasionally, until the mixture is dry on the top. Turn out onto a plate. Grease the pan lightly. Return the pancake-like mixture to the skillet and cook until golden on the other side. Cut into wedges and serve with the warm sauce. Serves 4.

Egg-Mushroom Curry from the East Indies

A different idea for a curry prepared with foods which are favorites in the East Indies. A superb brunch dish.

1 pound fresh mushrooms	2½ cups coconut milk*
5 tablespoons butter or oil	8 hard-cooked eggs, shelled
1 tablespoon fresh lemon juice	Condiments: grated coconut,
Salt, pepper to taste	sliced bananas, chutney,
½ cup minced onion	chopped peanuts and
2-3 teaspoons curry powder	chopped green onions
3 tablespoons flour	

Rinse the mushrooms quickly or wipe them with wet paper toweling to remove any dirt. Wipe dry and cut off any tough stem ends. Melt 3 tablespoons of butter in a large skillet. Add the lemon juice and mushrooms and sauté 5 minutes. Season with salt and pepper. Remove from the heat and set aside.

Melt 2 tablespoons of butter in a saucepan. Add the onion and curry powder and sauté until the onion is soft. Stir in the flour. Cook 1 minute. Gradually add the coconut milk and cook slowly, stirring, until the mixture is thick and smooth. Add the mushrooms and whole eggs and leave on the heat long enough to warm through. Serve, accompanied by the garnishes, in small bowls. Serves 4.

*Coconut milk: soak 2 cups dried coconut (unsweetened if available) in 2 cups water for 5 minutes, strain the liquid and use as milk.

Scrambled Eggs and Mushrooms from Hawaii

If you're looking for a different way of preparing scrambled eggs, try this flavorful combination. It is a good company dish for luncheon or brunch.

3 green onions, minced
2 tablespoons peanut oil
½ cup diced green pepper
1 jar or can (4 ounces) small
    whole mushrooms, drained
2-3 teaspoons soy sauce

Pepper to taste
¼ cup pineapple juice
1 cup drained pineapple
    chunks
8 eggs, slightly beaten

In a large skillet, sauté the green onions in the oil until tender. Add the green pepper, mushrooms, soy sauce and pepper and sauté 2 to 3 minutes. Combine the pineapple juice, chunks and eggs. Pour into the pan and mix well. Cook over low heat, stirring as for scrambled eggs, until set. Serve at once. Serves 4 as a luncheon dish.

Mushroom Quiche

The various French *quiches* which have become popular in America are often served for luncheons and early or late-evening suppers. This one is most pleasing to the eye and a pleasure to eat on any occasion.

8 slices bacon, cut into 1-inch
    pieces

Standard pastry for 1 crust
    9-inch pie

½ cup minced onion
3 tablespoons butter
½ pound fresh mushrooms,
    cleaned & sliced length-
    wise
1 tablespoon flour

1 cup grated Swiss cheese
4 large eggs, beaten
1¾ cups light cream or milk
Freshly grated nutmeg
Salt, pepper to taste

Cook the bacon until crisp; drain; set aside. Sauté the onion in the butter until tender. Add the mushrooms and sauté for 4 minutes. Mix in the flour and cook 1 minute. Remove from the stove and cool.

Roll out the pastry and arrange in a *quiche* pan or a 9-inch pie plate. Place the bacon over the crust. Top with the grated cheese. Then spoon the cooled mushroom mixture over it. Mix together the eggs, cream, nutmeg, salt and pepper and pour over the mushrooms. Bake in a preheated hot oven (425°F.) for 15 minutes. Reduce the heat to 300°F. and cook about 30 minutes longer, or until a knife inserted into the custard comes out clean. Serves 6. Let cool about 15 minutes before serving.

Baked Eggs and Mushrooms Mornay

1 pound fresh mushrooms
6 tablespoons butter
2 tablespoons lemon juice
6 hard-cooked eggs, shelled
¼ cup cooked peas
½ teaspoon turmeric powder

1 tablespoon mayonnaise
Salt, pepper to taste
3 tablespoons flour
1½ cups light cream or milk
¾ cup grated Swiss cheese

Rinse the mushrooms quickly or wipe them with wet paper toweling to remove any dirt. Wipe dry. Sauté in 3 tablespoons of butter and the lemon juice for 4 minutes, stirring once or twice. Remove from the heat.

Cut the eggs into halves lengthwise. Remove the yolks and mash with the peas. Mix in the turmeric, mayonnaise, salt and pepper. Spoon into the egg shells. Arrange in a buttered shallow baking dish leaving spaces between them. Spoon the mushrooms and drippings into the spaces.

Melt the remaining 3 tablespoons of butter in a saucepan. Stir in the flour to form a *roux*. Cook, stirring, 1 minute. Gradually add the cream, stirring, and cook, stirring, until thick and smooth. Mix in the cheese and cook slowly until it melts. Season with salt and pepper. Remove from the stove and pour over the stuffed eggs and mushrooms. Bake in a preheated moderate oven (350°F.) about 30 minutes, until hot and bubbly. Serves 6.

German Cheese-Mushroom Pudding

From the Germans we have acquired a flavorful accompaniment for roast poultry or meats, especially pork.

½ pound fresh mushrooms	2 tablespoons chopped fresh
3 tablespoons butter	parsley
1 medium onion, chopped	Dash nutmeg
2 tablespoons flour	Salt, pepper to taste
1 cup light cream or milk	3 eggs, separated
1 cup grated yellow cheese	Fine dry bread crumbs

Rinse the mushrooms quickly or wipe them with wet paper toweling to remove any dirt. Slice. Heat the butter in a saucepan. Add the onion and sauté until tender. Add the mushrooms and sauté for 4 minutes. Mix in the flour. Cook 1 minute. Add the cream, cheese, parsley, nutmeg, salt and pepper. Mix well and cook slowly, stirring, until the mixture is thickened and the cheese is melted. Remove from the stove. Stir some of the hot mixture into the egg yolks. Mix well and return to the mushroom combination. Beat the egg whites until stiff and fold into the mixture. Turn into a greased baking dish previously sprinkled with fine dry bread crumbs. Sprinkle the top with bread crumbs. Set in a dish of hot water. Bake in a preheated moderate oven (350°F.) for 45 minutes. Serves 4. Serve with Mushroom Sauce (page 206), if desired.

Hungarian Layered Mushroom Pancakes

The Hungarians are very fond of their many inventive dishes made with pancakes, *palacsinta*, which are filled with flavorful combinations of meats, poultry, cheeses and mushrooms or sweet mixtures for dessert. Many are rolled up after filling. In the recipe below, the pancakes however, are prepared and served in a tall stack.

Filling:	*Pancakes:*
1 *pound fresh mushrooms,*	2 *cups sifted all-purpose flour*
cleaned & chopped	1 *teaspoon salt*
3 *tablespoons butter*	3 *large eggs, beaten*
1 *teaspoon paprika*	2 *cups milk*
1 *cup sour cream*	*Grated Parmesan cheese*
1 *large egg, slightly beaten*	
Salt, pepper to taste	

For the filling, sauté the mushrooms in the butter for 4 minutes. Add the paprika and cook 1 minute. Stir in the sour cream, egg, salt and pepper. Remove from the heat and cool.

To make the pancakes, combine the flour, salt, eggs and milk in a bowl and mix with a whisk or spoon to blend thoroughly. Pour about ¼ cup of the batter into a greased 7 or 8 inch skillet and tilt at once to spread evenly. When cooked, turn over and fry on the other side. While cooking the others, keep the pancakes warm in the oven. (Makes about 10 pancakes) Arrange one in the bottom of a well greased shallow baking dish. Spread with some of the mushroom mixture. Repeat to use all the pancakes and filling. Do not spread the top one with the filling. Dot with butter and sprinkle with grated Parmesan. Cook in a preheated moderate oven (350°F.) about 20 minutes. To serve, cut into wedges. Serves 8.

Eggs à la Forestière

In French *forestière* means "of or pertaining to the forests." Dishes prepared *à la forestière* generally include those marvelous morels which grow in the forests and other foods such as bacon and potatoes. Another delicious luncheon entrée.

1 pound fresh mushrooms	Nutmeg, salt, pepper to taste
7 tablespoons butter or margarine	3 tablespoons flour
	2 cups milk
8 hard-cooked eggs, shelled	6 slices bacon, cut into 1-inch
2 tablespoons grated Parmesan cheese	pieces
	1 cup diced raw potatoes

Remove the stems from the mushrooms. Set aside the caps. Cut off any tough stem ends and chop the rest finely. Sauté in 2 tablespoons of butter for 3 minutes. Remove from the heat. Cut the eggs in half lengthwise. Remove the yolks and put in a small bowl. Add the sautéed mushrooms and drippings, the cheese, nutmeg, salt and pepper. Spoon into the egg whites. Arrange in a buttered shallow baking dish.

Melt 2 tablespoons of butter in a saucepan. Stir in the flour. Cook 1 minute. Gradually add the milk and cook slowly, stirring, until thick and smooth. Pour over and around the eggs.

Melt the remaining 3 tablespoons of butter in a skillet and

add the mushroom caps. Sauté for 4 minutes. Spoon over the sauce. Fry the bacon until crisp. Sprinkle over the mushrooms. Drain off all except 2 tablespoons of the fat. Fry the potatoes in it until tender. Spoon over the bacon. Heat the dish in a pre-heated moderate oven (375°F.) about 20 minutes, until hot and bubbly. Serves 4.

Mushroom Omelet, Shanghai Style

A flavorful omelet made with some favorite foods of the Chinese. Excellent for a late breakfast or brunch.

⅓ cup chopped green onions, with tops	1 cup diced celery
Peanut oil	½ cup diced bamboo shoots
1 cup sliced mushrooms, fresh or canned	Salt, pepper to taste
	6 eggs
	1-2 tablespoons soy sauce

Sauté the onions in 2 tablespoons of oil until soft. Add the mushrooms and sauté 2 minutes. Mix with the celery, bamboo shoots, salt and pepper. Turn into a bowl. Lightly beat the eggs. Add, with the soy sauce, to the mushroom mixture. Mix well. Grease an 8 inch skillet with peanut oil. Add the egg-mushroom mixture and tilt the pan to spread the ingredients evenly. Cook over low heat. Run a knife around the edge of the pan and tilt it so the liquid runs underneath. Continue cooking until the mixture is set and the top is dry. Fold over and serve. Serves 4.

English Mushroom-Cheese Tart

A good dish to serve for a light, late evening meal.

1 large onion, sliced	1 cup grated Cheddar cheese
1/4 pound butter	Freshly grated nutmeg
1½ pounds fresh mushrooms, cleaned & sliced	Salt, pepper to taste
2 tablespoons flour	2 tablespoons dry sherry
¾ cup light cream or milk	Pastry for 2-crust 9-inch pie

Sauté the onions in the butter until tender. Add the mushroom slices and sauté them for 5 minutes. Mix in the flour. Cook 1 minute. Stir in the cream and cheese and cook slowly, until the mixture thickens and the cheese is melted. Add the nutmeg, salt, pepper and sherry. Remove from the heat and cool.

Roll out slightly more than half of the pastry and line a 9-inch pie pan with it. Spoon in the mushroom-cheese mixture and spread evenly. Roll out the remaining pastry and cut into ½-inch strips. Arrange on the pie, lattice style. Wet the edge of the pie and place one strip around the edge. Press firmly with a fork to form a rim. Bake in a preheated hot oven (400°F.) about 30 minutes, until cooked. Serves 6.

Marvelous Mushroom Sandwiches

There are many excellent ideas for using mushrooms in sandwiches. Even children and teen-agers will find them inviting as they are different from the usual fare. Here are three of the many possibilities.

I.

½ cup chopped mushrooms,
  fresh or canned
1 tablespoon minced green
  onions
2 tablespoons butter or
  margarine

4 slices bacon, cut into 1-inch
  pieces
2 square slices yellow cheese
2 slices white bread

Sauté the mushrooms and green onions in the butter for 3 minutes. Fry the bacon until crisp and drain. Arrange the slices of cheese on the bread, spread lightly with butter, and mustard if desired. Top with the bacon and sautéed mushrooms and green onions. Put under the broiler long enough for the cheese to melt. Makes 2 sandwiches.

II.

¼ cup minced onions
3 tablespoons butter or
  margarine
½ cup diced cooked ham
1 pound fresh mushrooms,
  cleaned & sliced

6 eggs, lightly beaten
2 tablespoons chopped fresh
  parsley
Salt, pepper to taste
8 slices bread

Sauté the onions in the butter in a skillet until tender. Add the ham and mushrooms and sauté for 4 minutes. Add the eggs, parsley, salt and pepper and stir at once to mix well. Cook until the mixture is set and dry on top. Cut into 4 portions. Arrange each portion on a slice of bread. Top with another slice of bread. Spread the top with butter or margarine. Insert tooth picks to hold the sandwich together. Put under a grill until golden. Turn over. Butter the other side and grill it. Serve garnished with a cherry tomato and a small whole mushroom on a tooth pick. Makes 4 sandwiches.

III.

Combine diced cooked ham, mayonnaise, mustard, salt and pepper. Spread on a slice of rye bread. Top with a layer of thickly sliced raw mushrooms. Dot with butter and sprinkle with grated cheese. Cook in a preheated hot oven (400°F.) about 10 minutes.

Oeufs Mollet Chasseur

Eggs, prepared with a *chasseur sauce,* or "hunter's style," are enriched with shallots, tomatoes, white wine and mushrooms.

2 tablespoons minced shallots or green onions
3 tablespoons butter
1 cup sliced mushrooms, fresh or canned
2 medium tomatoes, peeled & chopped
⅓ cup dry white wine
Salt, pepper to taste
2 tablespoons chopped fresh parsley
4 eggs

Sauté the shallots in the butter until soft. Add the mushrooms and sauté 4 minutes. Add the tomatoes, wine, salt and pepper. Simmer slowly, covered, for 10 minutes. Stir in the parsley. Meanwhile, poach the eggs. Serve with the mushroom-tomato sauce spooned over and around the eggs. Serves 2 as a luncheon dish or 4 as a first course.

Italian Mushroom Frittata

The Italian omelet, or *frittata,* is a flat pancake-like dish filled with such ingredients as meats, poultry, vegetables, seafood,

or combination of them. This mushroom *frittata* is superb fare
for a brunch or luncheon.

2 *tablespoons olive oil*
4 *tablespoons butter*
1 *tablespoon minced onion*
1 *cup chopped mushrooms,*
   fresh or canned
⅓ *cup grated Parmesan*
   cheese

1 *tablespoon chopped fresh*
   herbs (basil, parsley,
   marjoram, tarragon)
6 *eggs*
Salt, pepper to taste

In a skillet heat the oil and 1 tablespoon of butter. Add the
onion and sauté until soft. Add the mushrooms and sauté for
3 minutes. Mix in the cheese and herbs and remove from
the stove. Beat the eggs lightly with a fork, just enough
to combine the yolks and whites. Add the mushroom mixture. Mix well. Heat 3 tablespoons of butter over high heat
in a 9-inch omelet pan or skillet and tip to coat the bottom and
sides. When slightly browned, pour in the egg mixture and tilt
the pan to spread evenly. Begin lifting up with a fork from the
sides as the eggs cook so the uncooked egg will run underneath.
When almost cooked, shake the pan back and forth so the eggs
do not stick. Toss lightly in the air to turn over. Or invert on
a large plate. Lightly grease the pan and return the egg mixture
to it. Cook the underside a few minutes. Slide onto a warm plate.
Serves 4.

Danish Mushroom Smørrebrød

The Danish open-faced sandwiches, *smørrebrød*, are made
with buttered bread covered with artistic and savory toppings.
They may be made with meats, vegetables, seafood, eggs, poultry
or combinations of them and then garnished. Some of the most

appealing of the sandwiches are those made with mushrooms. Included here are three easy-to-prepare suggestions which may be served for luncheon. Serve with knives and forks.

1. Spread slices of firm white bread generously with butter. Cover with slices of crisply fried bacon, one tomato slice, and sautéed mushroom slices. Sprinkle with chopped dill or parsley.

2. Spread slices of rye bread generously with butter. Cover with a thin slice of smoked salmon and a spoonful of chopped raw mushrooms mixed with mustard-flavored mayonnaise. Garnish with a sprig of parsley.

3. Spread slices of firm white or dark bread with butter. Place slices of cold cooked white chicken on the bread. Top each with canned whole mushrooms. Sprinkle with lemon juice and some chopped chives.

Swiss Chanterelles on Toast

The short-stemmed yellow wild mushrooms which the French call *chanterelles* have a most appealing flavor. They can be purchased in America either dried or in cans. Many of the latter are imported from Switzerland where they are treated, as they should be, with great respect.

1 can (4 ounces) chanterelles	Salt, freshly ground pepper to
6 tablespoons butter	taste
2 slices crustless white bread,	2 tablespoons flour
cut into halves	½ cup thick sweet or sour
2 tablespoons minced green	cream
onions	3 tablespoons grated Swiss
Freshly grated nutmeg to taste	cheese

Drain the *chanterelles* and cut into slices. Melt 4 tablespoons of the butter in a skillet and fry the bread in it on both sides. Remove and place in a buttered small shallow baking dish. Add the remaining butter to the pan and sauté the onions until tender. Add the *chanterelles* and sauté 4 minutes. Remove with a slotted spoon and arrange over the bread. Sprinkle with nutmeg, salt and pepper. Mix the flour into the butter drippings. Add the cream and mix well. Cook, stirring, over low heat until thickened and smooth. Pour over the *chanterelles*. Sprinkle with the cheese. Place in a preheated moderate oven (375°F.) for about 5 minutes. Serves 2.

Swiss Cheese Fondue with Mushrooms

The cheese fondue of Switzerland is eaten traditionally by dipping chunks of bread into the melted cheese. It can also be enjoyed with "dippers" such as fresh mushrooms or other vegetables. Serve it in a *caquelon*, the Swiss round earthenware casserole, or a similar utensil.

1 garlic clove	1 jigger kirsch or vodka
2 cups dry white wine	Dash nutmeg
½ pound Gruyère and	Freshly ground pepper
½ pound Emmentaler or 1	Cubes of crusty white bread
pound Swiss cheese,	Whole fresh mushrooms,
grated	cleaned
1 teaspoon cornstarch	

Rub the inside of a fondue dish or other cooking utensil with the garlic clove. Add the wine and put the dish over low heat. When just bubbling, add the grated cheese, a handful at a time, and the cornstarch mixed with the *kirsch*. Stir constantly with a wooden spoon until the cheese is melted and well mixed with the wine. Season with nutmeg and pepper. Let each guest dip the cubes of bread and mushrooms into the fondue with forks. Serves 6.

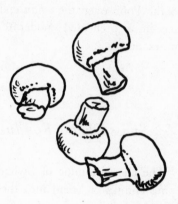

Huevos Española

The Spaniards have a vast repertoire of colorful and imaginative egg dishes such as this one, which includes their favorite seasonings of garlic, onions, olive oil, ham and fresh herbs.

1 small onion, minced
1 garlic clove, crushed
3 tablespoons olive or salad oil
⅓ cup chopped cooked ham
2 medium tomatoes, peeled & diced

1 cup chopped canned or fresh mushrooms
Salt, pepper to taste
6 eggs
2 tablespoons chopped fresh parsley

Sauté the onion and garlic in the oil until soft. Add the ham and fry. Mix in the tomatoes, mushrooms, salt and pepper and cook slowly, uncovered, for 10 minutes. Beat the eggs slightly and pour over the mushroom mixture. Stir and cook slowly until almost set. Stir in the parsley and cook a little longer. Serves 6.

Sherried Mushrooms and Eggs in Patty Shells

An excellent dish for a ladies' luncheon. Serve with a green salad.

2 tablespoons minced green onions	3 tablespoons flour
6 tablespoons butter	1½ cups light cream or milk
1 tablespoon lemon juice	6 hard-cooked eggs, peeled
1 pound fresh mushrooms cleaned & sliced or 1 can (8 ounces), drained	& diced
	3 tablespoons chopped fresh parsley
Dash nutmeg or mace	¼ cup dry sherry
Salt, pepper to taste	6 warm patty shells

Sauté the onions in 2 tablespoons of butter for 1 minute. Add the lemon juice and mushrooms and sauté 4 minutes if fresh, or 3 minutes if canned. Add the nutmeg, salt and pepper. Remove from the heat and set aside.

Melt the remaining 4 tablespoons of butter in a saucepan. Stir in the flour to form a *roux*. Cook, stirring, for 1 minute. Gradually add the cream, stirring as added, and cook slowly, stirring, until thick and smooth. Add the mushrooms and drippings, eggs, parsley and sherry, and leave on the stove long enough to heat through. Spoon into and around the warm patty shells and serve at once. Serves 6.

Easy Mushroom Party Pizza

This pizza is easy to prepare and may be frozen if desired. Reheat in a 450°F. oven about 10 minutes, or until the crust is golden and the sauce is bubbly.

Standard pizza pastry for
    12-inch pan
½ pound fresh mushrooms
2 tablespoons butter or
    margarine
2 cups tomato sauce

½ teaspoon dried oregano
Salt, pepper to taste
¼ pound Mozzarella cheese,
    thinly sliced
Grated Parmesan cheese

Roll out the pastry to about 13 inches in diameter. Shape in a pizza pan or other round dish. Clean the mushrooms and slice lengthwise through the stems. Sauté in the butter for 4 minutes. Remove from the heat. Pour the tomato sauce over the dough. Sprinkle with the oregano, salt and pepper. Arrange the Mozzarella slices on top. Put the sautéed mushrooms over them. Sprinkle with grated Parmesan. Bake in a preheated hot oven (425°F.) for 15 to 20 minutes. Cut into wedges. Serves 6.

Mushroom and Egg Ragoût Provençale

This is a colorful and savory dish to serve company which can be completely prepared beforehand and then slowly reheated.

1 tablespoon olive oil
2 tablespoons butter

3 medium tomatoes, peeled
    & chopped

1 *medium onion, chopped*   ½ *cup dry white wine*
1 *garlic clove, crushed*   *Salt, pepper to taste*
½ *pound fresh mushrooms,*   3 *tablespoons chopped parsley*
    sliced   6 *hard-cooked eggs, chopped*

Heat the oil and butter in a skillet. Add the onion and garlic and cook until soft. Add the mushrooms and sauté for 5 minutes. Mix in the tomatoes, wine, salt and pepper. Cook slowly, covered, for 10 minutes. Add the parsley and eggs and mix well. Simmer, covered, for 5 minutes. Serves 4.

Mushrooms Crêpes

Mushrooms and sour cream marry well in a number of inviting dishes including this one. A good brunch or luncheon creation.

1 *medium onion, finely*   2 *tablespoons chopped fresh*
    chopped   *parsley*
3 *tablespoons butter or*   *Freshly grated nutmeg*
    margarine   *Salt, pepper to taste*
1 *pound fresh mushrooms,*   1 *cup milk*
    cleaned & chopped   1 *large egg, beaten*
2 *tablespoons flour*   1 *cup sifted all-purpose flour*
½ *cup sour cream at room*   *Salt to taste*
    temperature   *Grated Parmesan cheese*

Sauté the onion in the butter until tender. Add the mushrooms and sauté for 5 minutes. Mix in the flour and cook 1 minute. Add the sour cream, parsley, nutmeg, salt and pepper. Cook slowly for 1 or 2 minutes to blend the flavors. Remove from the heat and cool.

Combine the milk, egg, flour and salt in a bowl and mix well with a whisk or fork to blend thoroughly. Pour about ¼ cup of the batter into a lightly greased 7 or 8 inch skillet. Tilt at once to spread evenly. Cook until brown on one side. Turn over and cook on the other side. Keep warm in the oven while cooking the others.

Spoon about 2 large spoonfuls of the mushroom mixture onto each pancake. Roll up and arrange, seam-side down, in a buttered shallow baking dish. Dot the top with butter and sprinkle with cheese. Put in a preheated hot (400°F.) oven for about 10 minutes before serving. Makes 8 to 10 crêpes.

Omelette aux Champignons

Such is the versatility of this long-time favorite that it may be served as a first course or as a light entrée for brunch, luncheon or supper.

3 tablespoons minced shallots or green onions	Freshly grated nutmeg
4 tablespoons butter	Salt, pepper to taste
½ pound sliced mushrooms, fresh or canned	6 eggs
2 tablespoons chopped fresh herbs	2 tablespoons light cream or milk

Sauté the shallots in 2 tablespoons of butter until tender. Add the mushrooms and sauté for 4 minutes. Add the herbs, nutmeg, salt and pepper. Keep warm.

With a fork mix the eggs lightly. Add the cream to them and season with salt and pepper. Melt the remaining 2 tablespoons of butter in an omelet pan or 8-inch skillet. Pour in the egg mixture and tilt to spread evenly. Cook over a low fire. When the mixture begins to set, loosen the edges and tilt to let the wet mixture run underneath. When almost cooked on the top, but still a little moist, spoon some of the warm mushroom mixture onto one side. Fold over and slide onto a warm plate. Cover with the remaining mushroom mixture. Serve at once. Serves 4.

Grains, Pasta and Rice

Fruits of the field, as cereals and grain are sometimes called, have been commonplace for so long that their gastronomic versatility is not always appreciated. In recent years, our menus have included more and more pasta and rice creations, but there is a wide variety of delectable and inviting dishes that can also be made with oats, wheat, barley, rye and corn. Mushrooms blend harmoniously to lend added allure to all of them.

Man's first cultivated crop, wheat, was developed from wild grasses growing in a Middle Eastern valley. The decision of ancient nomadic tribes to settle in permanent locales was certainly influenced by the necessity of planting and harvesting wheat and other early grains such as barley and rye. All early life evolved around these seasonal events which inspired ritual celebrations and holidays and influenced religious practices.

Probably the first dishes made with grain were flavorless potages. Gradually, however, the early cooks learned to make them more appealing by the addition of seasonings, nuts and fruits. Mushrooms were cultivated in ancient times but they were so highly prized that they were not eaten with other foods.

Thus, it was not until much later that Europeans devised interesting dishes combining grain and mushrooms. Eastern Europeans are fond of cooking their favorite barley and buckwheat groats with the additional flavor of wild or cultivated mushrooms. Rumanians and northern Italians add the fascinating fungi to their beloved corn-meal dishes. In southern Russia and the Middle East mushrooms make wholesome cracked wheat (*bulgur*) preparations more enticing.

In any number of cuisines rice dishes are enriched with magical mushrooms. They also have a particular affinity for the wide repertoire of pasta products, ranging from the familiar macaroni, noodles and spaghetti to the lesser known green noodles and *tagliatelle*.

This small collection of recipes is designed to exemplify the versatility and appeal of grain dishes enriched with marvelous mushrooms.

Risotto with Mushrooms

The very popular Northern Italian rice dish called *risotto* is richly flavored with saffron, cheese and white wine. Very often the regional wild mushrooms are also added to it. Cultivated ones, however, are good substitutes.

10 tablespoons butter	Salt, white pepper to taste
1 cup finely chopped onion	⅛ teaspoon saffron,
2 cups short or medium-grain	powdered or crumbled
rice	1 pound fresh mushrooms,
1 cup dry white wine	cleaned & sliced
2 cups (about) hot well-	½ cup freshly grated
seasoned chicken broth	Parmesan cheese

Melt 6 tablespoons of butter in a skillet. Add the onion and sauté until tender. Stir in the rice and sauté 5 minutes, or until the rice is well coated with butter. Turn the heat to high and pour in the wine. Add 1 cup of hot broth. Season with salt and pepper. Lower the heat a little and continue the cooking, un-covered, stirring frequently, until most of the liquid has been absorbed. Add the remaining liquid, ½ cup at a time, and continue cooking and stirring so the mixture does not stick to the pan. (Add more hot chicken broth, ½ cup at a time, if necessary.) The final rice should be tender but a little creamy. The cooking will take about 30 minutes or a little longer.

While the *risotto* is cooking, steep the saffron in a little hot water for a minute or two. Sauté the mushrooms in the remaining 4 tablespoons of butter. Mix the saffron, mushrooms and cheese into the *risotto*. Mix well but gently and serve. Serves 8.

Polish Barley-Mushroom Casserole

In Poland this dish is generally made with the very flavorful dried wild mushrooms. If available, they may be used in this recipe instead of cultivated mushrooms. Serve as an accompaniment to fish, meat or poultry.

⅓ cup butter	1 cup pearl barley
1 medium onion, chopped	3 cups boiling consommé
1 cup sliced mushrooms,	Salt, pepper to taste
fresh or canned	2 teaspoons chopped dill or
1 tablespoon lemon juice	parsley

Melt the butter in a heavy casserole or saucepan. Add the onion and sauté until tender. Mix in the mushrooms and lemon juice and sauté 3 minutes. Add the barley and sauté 1 minute. Pour in the consommé and bring to a boil. Season with salt and pepper. Lower the heat and cook slowly, tightly covered, about 1 hour, until the barley is tender and the liquid is absorbed. Stir in the dill. Makes 6 servings.

Swedish Mushroom Macaroni Pudding

A subtly flavored dish which in Sweden might be served with fish.

8 ounces macaroni elbows or
    twists
1 medium onion, chopped
2 tablespoons butter
1 tablespoon lemon juice
1 cup sliced mushrooms, fresh
or canned

Salt, white pepper to taste
2 teaspoons fresh dill
2 eggs, slightly beaten
1½ cups light cream or milk
Grated Parmesan cheese

Cook the macaroni in salted boiling water until tender; drain. While cooking, sauté the onion in the butter until tender. Add the lemon juice and mushrooms and sauté 4 minutes. Season with salt and pepper. Add the dill. Mix with the warm cooked macaroni and spoon into a greased baking dish. Combine the eggs and cream and pour over the mixture. Sprinkle the top with grated cheese. Dot with butter. Cook in a moderate oven (375°F.) for about 30 minutes. Serves 4.

Vermicelli with Peas and Mushrooms

Peas and mushrooms are a long-time favorite but gain new appeal when served over hot *vermicelli* (very thin spaghetti).

½ cup diced cooked ham
2 tablespoons olive oil
3 tablespoons butter

1 tablespoon lemon juice
2 cups green peas
½ teaspoon dried rosemary

¾ cup minced green onions
1-2 garlic cloves, crushed
2 cups whole button mush-
    rooms, fresh or canned

Salt; pepper to taste
½ pound cooked and drained
    vermicelli
Grated Parmesan cheese

Fry the ham with the oil, butter, onions and garlic until the onions are tender. Add the mushrooms and lemon juice and sauté 4 minutes. Stir in the peas, rosemary, salt and pepper and cook slowly, covered, until the peas are just tender. Serve over the hot *vermicelli*. Sprinkle with grated Parmesan. Serves 6.

Italian Polenta with Mushrooms

Maize or corn was introduced from the New World to Europe by the returning conquistadores. Neither corn nor the ground meal made from it was readily accepted as a food. Gradually, however, it became popular in northern Italy where, under the name of *polenta*, it is staple fare. It is eaten as a porridge or with sauces such as this one.

1 ounce dried mushrooms
¼ cup chopped onions
2 tablespoons olive oil
2 tablespoons tomato purée
1 cup canned tomatoes,
    chopped

2 teaspoons drained capers
½ teaspoon dried oregano
Salt, pepper to taste
2 cups water
1 cup yellow cornmeal
Grated Parmesan cheese

Soak the mushrooms in lukewarm water to cover for 20 minutes. Drain, pressing to release all the liquid. Slice.

Sauté the onions in the oil in a saucepan until tender. Add the tomato purée, tomatoes, capers, oregano, salt, pepper and sliced mushrooms. Cook slowly, uncovered, for 15 minutes.

Bring the water to a boil in a saucepan. Add 1 teaspoon

salt and gradually mix in the cornmeal, stirring constantly. Reduce the heat and continue the cooking, stirring, until the cornmeal thickens and comes away easily from the sides of the pan. Invert onto a platter. Cover with the warm tomato-mushroom sauce. Sprinkle with grated cheese. To serve, cut into wedges or slices. Serves 4.

Oriental Mushroom Fried Rice

A good brunch or supper dish.

3 tablespoons peanut oil
1 cup chopped green onions, with tops
1 cup chopped yellow onions
½ cup diced cooked ham

1½ cups sliced mushrooms, fresh or canned
3 cups cold cooked rice
4 eggs, slightly beaten
2 tablespoons soy sauce
Pepper to taste

Heat the oil in a Chinese *wok* or skillet. Add the onions and sauté until tender. Add the ham and mushrooms and sauté 3 minutes. Mix in the rice, eggs, soy sauce and pepper and cook slowly, stirring, until the eggs are cooked and the ingredients are heated. Serve at once. Serves 6.

Armenian Cracked Wheat Pilaf with Mushrooms

A staple grain in southern Russia and some parts of the Middle East is creacked wheat or *bulgur*, a small brown kernel which is actually hulled and pounded wheat. It has an appealing flavor and is most nutritious. *Bulgur* may be purchased in some super markets and specialty food stores.

5 tablespoons butter
1 medium onion, chopped
1½ cups chopped mush-
    rooms, fresh or canned
2 medium tomatoes, peeled
    & chopped

1 cup coarse cracked wheat
    (bulgur)
2½-3 cups beef bouillon
Salt, pepper to taste
2 tablespoons chopped fresh
    parsley

Melt 3 tablespoons of butter in a skillet and sauté the onion in it until tender. Add the mushrooms and sauté 3 minutes. Mix in the tomatoes and cracked wheat and cook slowly, stirring constantly, about 5 minutes. Add 2½ cups of bouillon, the salt and pepper, and bring to a boil. Lower the heat and cook slowly, covered, about 30 minutes, or until the cracked wheat is tender and the liquid is absorbed. Add more bouillon while cooking, if needed. Stir in the parsley and the remaining 2 tablespoons of butter. Serves 4.

Mushroom Brown Rice à l'Orange

One of the most nutritious of our packaged rices is the one called brown rice. It has an appealing nutty flavor but takes longer to cook than the white varieties. Serve this unusual dish with turkey or chicken.

1 medium onion, chopped
¼ cup butter
2 cans (4 ounces each)
    mushroom stems and
    pieces, drained
3 cups orange juice

1 cup packaged brown rice
⅓ cup almond slivers
⅓ cup seedless raisins
½ teaspoon dried marjoram
Salt, pepper to taste
Orange segments

Sauté the onion in the butter in a saucepan until tender. Add the mushrooms and sauté 1 minute. Pour in the orange juice and bring to a boil. Add the rice, almonds, raisins, marjoram, salt and pepper. Mix well. Lower the heat and cook slowly, covered, about 50 minutes, until the grains are tender and the liquid is absorbed. Do not stir while cooking. Serve garnished with orange segments. Serves 4.

Rice Mushroom Salad à la Française

An excellent dish for a summer meal served out of doors or inside. Prepare beforehand and keep ready in the refrigerator.

1 cup chopped canned or
  fresh mushrooms
3 tablespoons olive or salad
  oil
1 tablespoon fresh lemon juice
Salt, pepper to taste
2 cups cold cooked rice
1 cup cold cooked peas

½ cup chopped celery
¼ cup chopped canned
  pimiento
2 tablespoons chopped fresh
  herbs
Lettuce leaves
French dressing

Sauté the mushrooms in the oil and lemon juice for 3 minutes if canned, and 4 minutes if fresh. Season with salt and pepper. Remove from the heat and cool. In a large bowl mix with the rice, peas, celery, pimiento and herbs. Season with salt and pepper. Chill. Serve on lettuce leaves with French dressing. Serves 4.

German Baked Noodles and Mushrooms

For a company meal, prepare this dish beforehand and bake after guests arrive. It is a good accompaniment for pork, poultry or game.

8 ounces wide noodles
1 medium onion, minced
3 tablespoons melted butter
½ pound fresh mushrooms,
    cleaned & sliced
½ cup grated yellow cheese

1 egg, beaten
¾ cup light cream
Ground mace or freshly grated
    nutmeg
Salt, pepper to taste
Fine dry bread crumbs

Cook the noodles according to package directions; drain. While cooking, sauté the onion in the butter until tender. Add the mushrooms and sauté 4 minutes. Combine with the warm noodles in a buttered baking dish. Add the cheese and mix well. Combine the egg and cream and add, with the mace, salt and pepper, to the noodle mixture. Toss with two forks to combine well. Sprinkle the top with bread crumbs and dot with butter. Bake in a preheated moderate oven (350°F.), uncovered, for about 30 minutes or until golden on top. Serves 4 to 6.

Mushroom Noodles Smetana

The combination of mushrooms, noodles and sour cream is always a winner. It is particularly good when served with goulash.

½ pound medium egg
    noodles, broken
3 tablespoons butter or oil
2 tablespoons fresh lemon
    juice
1 cup sliced mushrooms,
    fresh or canned

1½ cups sour cream at
    room temperature
½ teaspoon paprika
Salt, pepper to taste
1 tablespoon chopped dill or
    parsley

Cook the noodles in boiling water until tender; drain. While cooking, heat the butter in a large saucepan. Add the lemon juice and mushrooms and sauté 4 minutes. Stir in the cooked noodles, sour cream, paprika, salt, pepper and dill. Toss with two forks to mix well. Serve at once. Serves 4.

Chinese Fried Noodles with Vegetables

A good supper dish for an informal occasion.

½ pound Chinese or Ameri-
  can egg noodles
Peanut or salad oil
1-2 tablespoons soy sauce
1 cup chopped green onions,
  with tops

2 cups sliced fresh mushrooms
1 package (6 ounces) frozen
  green pea pods (snow
  peas)
1 cup diced celery
⅓ cup sliced bamboo shoots

Cook the noodles in boiling salted water until just tender. Drain. In a large bowl mix the noodles with 2 tablespoons of oil and the soy sauce. Set aside.

Heat 2 tablespoons of oil in a Chinese *wok* or skillet. Add the onions and sauté until tender. Add the mushrooms, pea pods, celery and bamboo shoots. Cook slowly, stirring, until the vegetables are just tender. Add more oil while cooking, if necessary. With a slotted spoon, remove to a plate and keep warm. Put the noodles in the skillet and fry in oil until crisp. Return the vegetables to the pan and leave on the stove long enough to warm through. Serves 6.

Mushroom Kasha from Russia

The most popular grain dish in Russia is called *kasha* and is generally prepared with buckwheat groats. These are sold in packages in America called *kasha*. Buckwheat groats are flavorful, nourishing and inexpensive. Favorite flavorings for them are mushrooms and sour cream.

1 cup buckwheat groats (kasha)	1 medium onion, chopped
1 egg	1½ cups chopped or sliced mushrooms, fresh or canned
1 teaspoon salt	
2 cups boiling bouillon	1 cup sour cream, at room temperature
¼ cup butter	

Combine the buckwheat groats with the egg and salt in a heavy saucepan and cook, stirring constantly, for 1 minute or until grains are separate and dry. Add the hot bouillon and cook slowly, tightly covered, for about 30 minutes, or until the groats are done.

While cooking, heat the butter in a small saucepan. Add the onion and sauté until tender. Add the mushrooms and sauté 4 minutes. When the buckwheat groats are cooked, stir in the mushroom mixture and the sour cream. Serve as an accompaniment. Serves 6.

Macaroni Mushroom Zucchini Timballo

In Italy, pasta is often cooked with other ingredients in a pastry shell called a *timballo*. There is a special mold for its preparation. This dish is a variation which can be easily made in American kitchens.

2 pie crust sticks
2 cups macaroni elbows
½ cup chopped green onions
3 tablespoons butter or margarine

2 cans (8 ounces) button mushrooms, drained
1 can (1 pound) zucchini in tomato sauce
½ cup grated Parmesan cheese

Prepare 1 pie crust stick according to package instructions. Roll out the dough and line a 9" x 1½" round cake pan with it. Cook the macaroni in boiling salted water until tender. Drain. Sauté the green onions in the butter in a saucepan until tender. Add the mushrooms and sauté 3 minutes. Add the zucchini, including the tomato sauce, and heat. Stir in the macaroni and spoon into the pastry-lined cake pan. Sprinkle the top with the grated Parmesan. Prepare and roll out the remaining pastry stick and fit over the top of the dish. Make several slits in the pastry. Bake in a preheated moderate oven (375°F.) for 30 to 40 minutes, until the pastry is cooked. To serve, cut into wedges. Serves 6 to 8.

Viennese Egg Noodle Ring with Creamed Mushrooms

An excellent luncheon dish which can be prepared beforehand and re-heated after guests arrive.

12 ounces medium wide egg noodles
3 tablespoons butter, melted
3 eggs, separated

2 tablespoons chopped fresh parsley
Salt, pepper to taste
4 cups creamed mushrooms

2 *cups sour cream at room*
   temperature

Cook the noodles until soft and drain. Turn into a large bowl. Combine the melted butter and egg yolks and stir to mix well. Add to the sour cream. Stir in the parsley, salt and pepper and mix well. Mix with the noodles, tossing with two forks to combine well. Beat the egg whites until stiff and fold into the noodle mixture. Spoon into a greased 6½ cup ring mold. Place in a pan of hot water. Bake in a preheated moderate oven (375°F.) about 40 minutes, until firm. Unmold onto a warm platter. Fill the center and surround the ring with the creamed mushrooms (recipe below). Serves 8 to 10.

Creamed Mushrooms

2 *pounds fresh mushrooms*   2 *cups light sweet cream or*
½ *cup butter*   *sour cream*
2 *tablespoons lemon juice*   *Salt, white pepper to taste*
¼ *cup flour*

Clean the mushrooms. Wipe dry. Sauté in the butter and lemon juice in a large saucepan for 4 minutes. Stir in the flour and mix well. Gradually add the cream and cook slowly, stirring, until thickened. Season with salt and pepper.

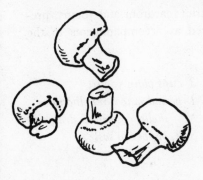

Korean Mushroom Rice

This is a good accompaniment for beef, particularly barbecued ribs or steaks.

1 cup sliced green or yellow
   onions
3 tablespoons peanut oil
1 cup sliced mushrooms,
   fresh or canned
2 tablespoons soy sauce

Freshly ground pepper
1 tablespoon toasted sesame
   seeds*
3 cups bouillon or water
1½ cups uncooked medium-
   grain rice

Sauté the onions in the oil until soft. Add the mushrooms, soy sauce, pepper and sesame seeds and cook 2-3 minutes. Add the bouillon and mix well. Bring to a boil. Stir in the rice and lower the heat. Cook slowly, tightly covered, or until the grains are tender and the liquid is absorbed, about 30 minutes. Do not stir while cooking. Serves 6.

*Fry in a skillet until brown.

Mushroom Macaroni with Yogurt

In the Middle Eastern countries macaroni and yogurt, prepared in various forms, are served as accompaniments to the favorite meat which is lamb.

1 large onion, chopped
1-2 garlic cloves, crushed
4 tablespoons olive or salad
   oil

3 cups plain yogurt
1 pound macaroni elbows or
   shells, cooked & drained
Salt, pepper to taste

2 cups sliced mushrooms,   ¼ cup chopped parsley
   fresh or canned   3 tablespoons melted butter
1 tablespoon lemon juice   2 teaspoons paprika

Sauté the onion and garlic in the oil in a saucepan until tender. Add the mushrooms and lemon juice and sauté 3 minutes. Pour in the yogurt. Add the cooked macaroni, salt and pepper and cook gently until warmed through. Stir in the parsley. Serve with the melted butter and paprika mixed together as a garnish. Serves 8.

Caucasian Plov with Mushrooms

In Southern Russia popular rice dishes are called *plov* and are made with a variety of ingredients including meats, poultry, vegetables, fruits and nuts. Serve this one with such Russian favorites as *shashlik* (shish kebab), braised chicken or meat-stuffed cabbage leaves.

1 cup dried apricots   1 cup sliced mushrooms,
½ cup seedless raisins   fresh or canned
¼ teaspoon ground saffron   3 cups chicken broth
3 tablespoons butter   1½ cups uncooked rice
                                 Salt, pepper to taste

Cover the apricots and raisins with boiling water and soak 2 hours. Drain; slice the apricots. Steep the saffron in 2 tablespoons of hot water. Melt the butter in a saucepan. Add the mushrooms and sauté for 3 minutes. Pour in the broth and bring to a boil. Stir in the rice, apricots, raisins and saffron. Season with salt and pepper. Lower the heat and cook slowly, covered, about 25 minutes, until the rice grains are tender and the liquid is absorbed. Serves 8.

Vegetable Pilau à l'Indienne

A colorful dish to serve with meatballs or roast lamb.

1 large onion, chopped
1-2 garlic cloves, crushed
3 tablespoons butter
1 teaspoon ground turmeric
½ teaspoon cayenne
½ teaspoon ground ginger
½ teaspoon ground cumin
Salt, pepper to taste

2 cups sliced mushrooms,
*   fresh or canned*
2 medium tomatoes, peeled &
*   chopped*
½ cup cooked diced carrots
1 cup cooked peas
2 cups cooked rice
2 cups plain yogurt

Sauté the onion and garlic in the butter in a large saucepan until soft. Add the spices, salt and pepper. Cook 1 minute. Add the mushrooms and sauté 3 minutes. Stir in the tomatoes and cook slowly, covered, for 10 minutes. Add the remaining ingredients and leave on low heat long enough to warm through. Serves 4 to 6.

Baked Green Noodles and Mushrooms à la Crème

This is an excellent entrée for a women's luncheon or may be served as an accompaniment to chicken, turkey or duckling.

¼ cup minced onions
3 tablespoons butter
½ pound fresh mushrooms,
*   sliced*
1 tablespoon lemon juice

1 cup grated Swiss cheese
Freshly grated nutmeg
Salt, pepper to taste
8 ounces green or spinach
*   noodles*

3 tablespoons flour   Fine dry bread crumbs
2 cups light cream

Sauté the onions in the butter until tender. Add the mushrooms and lemon juice and sauté for 4 minutes. Stir in the flour.
Gradually add the cream and cook slowly, stirring, until thickened.
Add the cheese, nutmeg, salt and pepper and cook until the
cheese is melted. Remove from the heat.

Cook the noodles until just tender; drain. Spoon into a
buttered shallow baking dish. Top with the mushroom mixture.
Sprinkle the top with bread crumbs and dot with butter. Put on
the top shelf of a preheated hot (425°F.) oven for about 10
minutes, until golden. Serves 4 to 6.

Mushroom Chow Mein

The popular dish we call chow mein was probably created
by a Chinese American but a similar one is served in China.
There, however, the spelling is *chao mien*. This home-made version is an excellent supper dish and may be served over the canned
crisp noodles.

2 cups sliced onions   1 teaspoon chopped ginger
½ cup peanut oil   (optional)
1 pound fresh mushrooms,   ¼ cup cornstarch
    cleaned & sliced   ½ cup soy sauce
    lengthwise   2 cups water
2 cups chopped celery   Pepper to taste
½ cup bamboo shoots   Chow mein noodles
2 cups bean sprouts, drained

Sauté the onions in the oil in a large skillet until tender.
Add the mushrooms and sauté 2 minutes. Add the celery and
bamboo shoots and sauté another 2 minutes. Mix in the bean

sprouts and ginger. Dissolve the cornstarch in the soy sauce. Add, with the water, to the mushroom mixture. Cook slowly, stirring, until slightly thickened. Serve at once over hot chow mein noodles. Serves 8.

Mushroom Mamaliga from Rumania

Cornmeal, or *mamaliga*, is the most beloved food in Rumania and is cooked and served in various ways. Sometimes it is eaten as a porridge or it is made into dishes such as this one.

3 cups water	Grated yellow cheese
1 teaspoon salt	Butter
1 cup yellow cornmeal	Fine dry bread crumbs
2 cups sautéed mushrooms	

Bring the water to a boil. Add the salt. Slowly add the cornmeal and stir vigorously until the mixture is thick and smooth and comes away easily from the sides of the pan. Spoon half of it into a buttered casserole. Cover with 1 cup of the sautéed mushrooms and a good sprinkling of grated cheese. Dot with butter. Repeat the layers of cornmeal, mushrooms and cheese. Top with a sprinkling of bread crumbs and dot with butter. Bake in a preheated moderate oven (350°F.) for about 30 minutes, until golden brown. Serves 4 to 6.

Mushroom Wild Rice

1 cup uncooked wild rice	½ pound sliced fresh
4 cups water	mushrooms
1 teaspoon salt	½ teaspoon dried oregano
3 tablespoons butter	½ teaspoon dried marjoram
1 medium onion, minced	Salt, pepper to taste

Wash the rice several times in cold water. Put the water in a saucepan and bring to a boil. Add the salt. Gradually add the rice while the water is still boiling. Lower the heat and cook slowly, covered, about 35 minutes, or until the grains are tender and the water is absorbed.

While cooking, melt the buter in a skillet. Add the onion and sauté until tender. Add the mushrooms and sauté 5 minutes. Stir in the herbs, salt and pepper. Mix with the cooked wild rice. Serves 6 to 8.

Spaghetti con Funghi

This rich mushroom combination is a most flavorful sauce to serve over hot spaghetti and it is easy to prepare.

4 bacon strips, chopped
2 tablespoons olive oil
1 large onion, chopped
1-2 garlic cloves, crushed
½ pound sliced fresh
    mushrooms
2 medium, fresh tomatoes,
    peeled & chopped, or
    2 canned Italian-style
    tomatoes, chopped

1 tablespoon chopped fresh
    herbs (basil, tarragon,
    parsley, marjoram)
Salt, pepper to taste
½ pound cooked spaghetti,
    drained
Grated Parmesan cheese

Fry the bacon in a skillet until crisp. Pour off all except 1 tablespoon of the fat. Add the oil and heat. Add the onion and garlic and sauté until soft. Stir in the mushrooms and sauté 3 minutes. Stir in the tomatoes, herbs, salt and pepper. Cook slowly, covered, for 10 minutes. To serve, spoon over the hot cooked spaghetti. Sprinkle with grated Parmesan. Serves 4.

Seafood

We Americans are indeed fortunate that our country has a bountiful harvest of foods from the sea. The yield of fish and shellfish from the lovely blue waters of our surrounding oceans and gulfs, inland lakes, rivers and streams provides us with great variety throughout the year. Since the natural flavor of each fresh or salt water denizen should be preserved, only foods that enhance it should be cooked with seafood. Mushrooms are perfect companions for this fare.

Since the settling of our country, seafood has been most important for daily meals and company fare. The early colonists might not have survived without the abundance of cod in New England, crabs and oysters in Maryland, trout and whitefish from the Great Lakes, catfish in the south, and salmon and smelts in the northwest, to name only a few.

In those early days, and for many decades thereafter, our forefathers were limited to seafood taken from local waters. Also, unless salted or otherwise preserved, fish was enjoyed only in season. Today, due to modern transportation, preservation and packaging, we can relish all varieties from across the land. Fresh, frozen or canned, the supply of seafood is intriguing, abundant and readily available.

Except for some shellfish specialties, seafood is inexpensive. All is nutritious and a welcome change of pace from meats and poultry. Unlike yesteryear, there is no cleaning problem as it will already have been done or can be quickly accomplished by the experts in the super-markets. The flesh is tender and does not require a long cooking period. Seafood is very often cooked with such flavorings as butter, wine, lemon juice, herbs and mushrooms but may also be combined with a wide number of other foods.

From the cooks of the world we have fortunately inherited a marvelous repertoire of seafood recipes. These range from our own favorite regional specialties to those devised by seafood fanciers in Europe and the Orient. Whether steamed, stewed, broiled, baked or fried, each is an inviting preparation.

With this small collection, one can readily comprehend the appeal of combining mushrooms with our marvelous marine delicacies.

Coquilles Saint Jacques au Champagne

In France the name for one variety of scallop is *Coquille Saint Jacques,* but we have adopted the name for a flavorful dish made with scallops in a creamy sauce and served in shells. This is a Belgian variation.

1 cup dry champagne	Juice of 1 lemon
2 tablespoons minced shallots or green onions	½ pound fresh mushrooms, cleaned & sliced
3 sprigs parsley	Freshly grated nutmeg
⅛ teaspoon dried thyme	2 tablespoons flour
Salt, freshly ground pepper to taste	1 cup heavy cream
	⅓ cup buttered bread crumbs
1 pound sea scallops, washed & diced	2 tablespoons grated Parmesan cheese
4 tablespoons butter	

Combine the champagne, shallots, parsley, thyme, salt and pepper in a saucepan and bring to a boil. Add the scallops and lower the heat. Cook slowly, covered, until the scallops are tender, about 5 minutes. Remove from the stove and spoon out the scallops. Strain the liquid and set aside.

Melt 2 tablespoons of butter in a skillet. Add the lemon juice and mushrooms and sauté for 4 minutes. Season with nutmeg, salt and pepper. Remove from the heat and spoon out the mushroms, adding to the scallops. Add the drippings to the champagne broth and bring to a rapid boil. Cook until the liquid is reduced to 1 cup.

Melt 2 tablespoons of butter in a saucepan. Stir in the flour and cook 1 minute. Pour in the reduced liquid and cook slowly, stirring, until it becomes a thick and smooth sauce. Add the cream and bring to a quick boil. Remove at once from the heat. Add the scallops and mushrooms. Spoon into six individual shells or ramekins. Sprinkle with the buttered crumbs and grated cheese. Put under the broiler and leave about 5 minutes, or until bubbly and golden on top. Serves 6.

Mediterranean Fish Stew with Mushrooms

Serve from a handsome tureen for an early supper or late evening meal.

2 medium onions, sliced
1-2 garlic cloves, crushed
⅓ cup olive oil
1 can (29 ounces) tomatoes
1 large bay leaf
½ teaspoon dried basil
3 sprigs parsley
1 cup dry white wine
3 pounds mixed cleaned fish,
    cut into serving pieces

3 anchovy fillets, cut up
Pepper to taste
1 pound whole fresh
    mushrooms, cleaned
3 tablespoons butter
1 tablespoon lemon juice
¼ cup chopped fresh parsley
Slices of crusty white bread

Sauté the onions and garlic in the oil in a kettle or large saucepan until tender. Add the tomatoes, bay leaf, basil, and parsley and cook 5 minutes. Add the wine, fish, anchovies and pepper. Pour in enough water to cover. Cook over fairly high heat until the fish is just tender, about 12 minutes. While cooking, sauté the mushrooms in the butter and lemon juice for 5 minutes. Add, with the parsley, to the stew. Correct the seasoning. Discard the bay leaf and parsley sprigs. Spoon the fish, mushrooms and broth on the crusty bread slices in large soup bowls. Serves 6.

Colonial Mushroom Oyster Pie

A culinary gift from our forefathers who relished rich seafood pies. Mushrooms and oysters are most agreeable fare.

1 pound fresh mushrooms	*Dash cayenne*
½ cup butter	*Freshly grated nutmeg, salt*
1 small onion, grated	*and ground pepper to*
1 tablespoon lemon juice	*taste*
1 pint oysters	*2 tablespoons dry sherry*
3 tablespoons flour	*Pie or other rich pastry*
1½ cups light cream	

Clean and slice the mushrooms. Melt ¼ cup of the butter in a skillet. Add the mushrooms, onion and lemon juice. Sauté for 4 minutes. Cook the oysters in their own liquor about 5 minutes or until their edges begin to curl. Drain, reserving the liquid.

Melt the remaining ¼ cup of butter in a saucepan. Mix in the flour to form a *roux* and cook for 1 minute. Gradually add the cream and reserved oyster liquid and cook slowly, stirring, until the sauce is thickened and smooth. Add the cayenne, nutmeg, salt and pepper. Stir in the sherry. Remove from the heat. Spoon the sautéed mushrooms and the oysters into a buttered shallow baking dish. Pour the sauce over them. Top with the pastry. Cut slits in it for steam to escape. Bake in a preheated hot oven (450°F.) about 15 minutes, until the top is golden. Serves 6.

Fillets of Fish Bonne Femme

Our gastronomic labels sometimes have strange meanings. *Bonne femme*, for example, means in French, "a good wife". In cooking, however, it refers to a preparation of ingredients with mushrooms and white wine.

1½ pounds fish fillets (bass, cod, flounder, haddock, perch)	½ pound fresh mushrooms, cleaned & sliced
Salt, pepper	1 tablespoon lemon juice
1 medium onion, minced	2 tablespoons chopped fresh parsley
1 garlic clove, crushed	½ cup dry white wine
4 tablespoons butter or margarine	¼ cup light cream
	1 teaspoon flour

Sprinkle the fillets with salt and pepper. Sauté the onion and garlic in 3 tablespoons of butter in a small skillet until tender. With a slotted spoon, remove to a large skillet. Place the fillets over them. Add the mushrooms and lemon juice to the drippings in the small skillet and sauté for 4 minutes. Spoon over the fish, adding the liquid also. Sprinkle with parsley. Pour the wine around the fish. Bring to a boil. Lower the heat and cook slowly, covered, about 7 minutes, or until the fish are just tender. Add the remaining tablespoon of butter to the pan. Stir in the flour. Gradually add the cream and cook slowly, stirring, until thickened. Serve at once. Serves 4.

Swiss Trout with Mushroom Stuffing

Serve for a weekend luncheon with hot buttered rice and a green salad.

6 *fresh or frozen trout*
Salt
½ *cup sliced green onions*
⅔ *cup butter or margarine*
2 *cups sliced mushrooms,*
   fresh or canned

1 *tablespoon lemon juice*
4 *cups soft bread cubes*
½ *teaspoon dried marjoram*
¼ *cup chopped fresh parsley*
Pepper to taste

If frozen trout are used, thaw them. Clean, wash and dry. Sprinkle inside and outside with salt. Sauté the onions in ½ cup of butter in a skillet until tender. Add the mushrooms and lemon juice and sauté for 4 minutes. Add the bread cubes and sauté until golden. Stir in the marjoram and parsley. Season with salt and pepper. Spoon into the fish cavities. Close with small skewers. Arrange in 1 or 2 buttered shallow baking dishes. Brush with remaining butter. Bake, uncovered, in a preheated moderate oven (350°F.) about 25 minutes, or until fork tender. Serves 6.

Easy Mushroom Seafood Casserole

A good dish for an impromptu meal.

1 *pound fresh mushrooms*
5 *tablespoons butter*
3 *tablespoons flour*

1 *can (5 ounces) shrimp,*
   deveined
Fine dry bread crumbs

2 *cups light cream or milk*　　*1 can (6½ to 7 ounces)*
⅛ *teaspoon nutmeg*　　　　　　*crabmeat, cleaned*
Salt, pepper to taste　　　　*Grated Parmesan cheese*

Clean the mushrooms and cut off any tough stem ends. Carefully pull the stems from the caps. Chop the stems and set aside. Sauté the caps in the butter in a saucepan for 4 minutes. Remove with a slotted spoon to a plate. Add the chopped stems to the drippings and sauté for 3 minutes. Stir in the flour and blend well. Gradually add the cream and cook slowly, stirring, until thickened. Add the nutmeg, salt and pepper. Stir in the shrimp and crabmeat and cook 1 minute to blend the flavors.

Arrange the mushroom caps, except 5 of them, in a buttered shallow baking dish. Spoon the seafood and sauce over them. Sprinkle the top with bread crumbs and cheese. Decorate the top with the 5 mushroom caps. Put in a preheated hot oven (425°F.) for about 15 minutes or until hot and bubbly. Serves 6.

West Coast Salmon-Mushroom Salad

A good main dish salad for a summer luncheon.

1 *can (1 pound) salmon,*　　　½ *cup sliced radishes*
　　cleaned & drained　　　　1 *cup (about) mayonnaise*
2 *cups cold cooked rice*　　　2 *tablespoons lemon juice*
1 *cup chopped celery*　　　　1 *tablespoon curry powder*
1 *cup canned sliced*　　　　　*Salt, pepper to taste*
　　mushrooms

Flake the salmon and combine in a large bowl with the rice, celery, mushrooms and radishes. Mix the mayonnaise, lemon juice, curry powder, salt and pepper and fold into the salmon mixture. Chill. Serve on lettuce leaves. Serves 6.

Lobster Mushroom Thermidor

Regal fare to serve at an elegant, intimate meal.

3 boiled lobsters, about 1 pound each	Dash cayenne
3 tablespoons butter	Salt, pepper to taste
2 tablespoons flour	½ pound fresh mushrooms, previously sautéed
1 cup light cream	Fine dry bread crumbs
Freshly grated nutmeg	Grated Parmesan cheese

Split the lobsters and remove the meat. Clean and rinse the shells. Cut the lobster into small pieces. Melt the butter in a saucepan. Stir in the flour to form a *roux*. Cook 1 minute. Gradually add the cream and cook slowly, stirring, until thick and smooth. Season with nutmeg, cayenne, salt and pepper. Mix in the lobster and mushrooms and leave on the stove just long enough to heat through. Spoon into the cleaned lobster shells. Sprinkle the tops with bread crumbs and cheese. Put on the top shelf of a preheated hot oven (400°F.) for about 10 minutes, until golden on top. Serves 4.

Danish Fish Gratiné

The Danes prepare delectable dishes with their rich bounty of seafood. Many are flavored with mushrooms. This one has a golden flavorful crust or *"gratin"*.

1 pound cod or flounder fillets	½ pound sliced fresh mushrooms

2 lemon slices

1 bay leaf

3 sprigs parsley

3 whole peppercorns

3 tablespoons butter

2 tablespoons flour

Freshly grated nutmeg

Salt, pepper to taste

1/4 cup dry sherry

Fine dry bread crumbs

Grated Parmesan cheese

Put the fish fillets in a large saucepan. Add the lemon slices, bay leaf, parsley and peppercorns. Pour in 2½ cups of water. Bring to a boil. Reduce the heat and cook slowly, covered, about 10 minutes, until the fish is just tender. Remove the fish and keep warm. Strain the broth and reserve.

Melt the butter in a saucepan. Add the mushrooms and sauté 4 minutes. Mix in the flour and cook 1 minute. Gradually add 2 cups of the strained broth. Cook slowly, stirring, until the sauce is thickened. Season with nutmeg, salt and pepper. Stir in the sherry and remove from the heat.

Spoon the cooked fish into a buttered baking dish. Spoon the mushrooms and sauce over the fish. Sprinkle the top generously with the bread crumbs and cheese. Set on the top shelf of a pre-heated hot oven (425°F.) for about 12 minutes, or until the top is golden. Serves 4.

Tuna Nicoise

An easy-to-prepare dish for a family supper.

1 medium onion, chopped

1-2 garlic cloves, crushed

3 tablespoons olive oil

1 can (8 ounces) mushroom
   stems and pieces

1 can (1 pound) tomatoes

1/2 teaspoon dried oregano

Salt, pepper to taste

2 tablespoons chopped parsley

12 pitted black olives

2 cans (about 7 ounces each)
   tuna, drained

Sauté the onion and garlic in the oil in a saucepan until tender. Add the mushrooms and sauté 3 minutes. Mix in the tomatoes, oregano, salt and pepper and cook slowly, covered, for 15 minutes. Mix in the parsley, olives and tuna and leave on the stove long enough to heat through. Serves 4 to 6.

English Sole with Mushrooms

The English are devotees of their flavorful channel or Dover sole which is known for its delicate flesh. True sole is found only in European waters. American "sole" is actually other flat fish, usually flounder. "Gray sole" is one of the best varieties of flounder.

1 pound gray sole or other flounder fillets
2 tablespoons softened butter
2 tablespoons chopped parsley
2 tablespoons chopped chives
Freshly grated nutmeg and ground pepper to taste
¼ cup white wine

¼ pound fresh mushroom caps
3 tablespoons butter
1 tablespoon lemon juice
1 can (5 ounces) shrimp, deveined & drained
½ cup heavy cream
1 teaspoon anchovy paste
2 egg yolks

Arrange the fillets in a buttered shallow baking dish. Combine the softened butter, parsley and chives and mash with a fork. Form into 1-inch balls. Place over the fillets. Sprinkle with the nutmeg and pepper. Pour the wine into the dish. Bake, covered with foil, in a preheated moderate oven (350°F.) about 12 minutes, or until fork tender.

While cooking, clean the mushroom caps and wipe dry. In a saucepan sauté them in 2 tablespoons of butter and the lemon juice for 4 minutes. Stir in the shrimp. Remove from the heat.

When the fish fillets are cooked, spoon off the juices at once. Mix with the remaining 1 tablespoon of butter in a small saucepan. Add the cream and anchovy paste and heat through. Remove from the stove and stir in the egg yolks, mixing with a fork. Spoon the mushroom-shrimp mixture over the warm fish fillets. Top with the cream sauce. Place under the broiler for about 5 minutes. Serves 4.

Crabmeat and Mushrooms in a Spinach Ring

Serve for a ladies' luncheon. The ring and seafood sauce can both be prepared beforehand. The dish is pretty to look at and delightful to savor.

3 packages (10 ounces each) frozen chopped spinach
6 tablespoons (about) butter
5 tablespoons flour
2½ cups milk
Freshly grated nutmeg
Salt, pepper to taste

3 eggs, beaten
1 pound fresh mushrooms
½ cup light cream
¼ teaspoon cayenne pepper
2 tablespoons dry sherry
2 cans (6½ or 7 ounces each) crabmeat

Cook the spinach; drain. Chop finely. Melt 2 tablespoons of butter in a saucepan. Stir in 2 tablespoons of flour to form a *roux*. Cook 1 minute. Gradually add 1 cup of milk and cook slowly, stirring, until the sauce is thickened and smooth. Season with nutmeg, salt and pepper. Add the spinach and eggs and mix well. Spoon into a buttered 6 cup ring mold. Place in a pan of hot water and bake in a preheated moderate oven (350°F.) about 1 hour, or until firm.

While the ring is cooking, clean and dry the mushrooms.

Carefully pull the stems from the caps. Sauté the caps in about ⅓ cup of butter for 4 minutes. Sauté a few at a time and add more butter, if needed. Remove from the stove and set aside. (Use the stems in another dish).

Melt 2 tablespoons of butter in a saucepan. Stir in 3 tablespoons of flour and cook 1 minute. Gradually add 1½ cups of milk and the cream. Cook slowly, stirring, until thickened and smooth. Stir in the mushrooms, cayenne, sherry and crabmeat. Season with salt and pepper. Leave on the stove long enough to heat through. When the spinach ring is cooked, unmold on a warm platter. Spoon the crabmeat-mushroom mixture in the center of the ring and around it. Serves 6 to 8.

Mediterranean Fish-Stuffed Mushrooms

The very large mushroom caps are not always available, but they are delightful for stuffing with flavorful creations such as this one. A good luncheon dish.

12 extra-large fresh mush- rooms or 18 large ones	*⅔ cup minced cooked white fish*
⅓ cup (about) olive oil	*2 tablespoons dry white wine*
½ cup butter or margarine	*¼ cup chopped fresh parsley*
¼ cup minced green onions, with tops	*Pinch dried basil*
2 garlic cloves, crushed	*Salt, pepper to taste*
	Grated Parmesan cheese

Clean the mushrooms and wipe dry. Carefully pull the stems from the caps. Mince the stems. Sauté the caps on both sides in the oil and butter. Remove and place in a shallow baking dish. Sauté the onions and garlic in the drippings, adding more oil if needed, until tender. Stir in the minced stems and sauté until tender. Add the fish, wine, parsley, basil, salt and pepper and cook about 4 minutes to blend the flavors. Spoon into the mushroom caps. Sprinkle with Parmesan and dot with butter. Put under the broiler for about 5 minutes before serving. Serves 4.

Mushroom-Stuffed Fish Steaks from the Northwest

Alaska, Oregon and Washington have a bountiful seafood harvest which for many years was only available locally. Today it can be enjoyed throughout the nation. Two of the best known fish from this region are halibut and salmon, sold in large flavorful steaks.

2 steaks or fillets of halibut or salmon, about 1 pound each	½ pound sliced fresh mushrooms
Salt, pepper to taste	1 cup soft bread cubes
¼ cup chopped green onions	⅓ cup chopped fresh parsley
6 tablespoons butter	1 tablespoon milk
	1 lemon, sliced

Remove any skin from the fish steaks. Sprinkle both sides with salt and pepper. Place 1 steak in a buttered shallow baking dish. Spoon the stuffing (recipe below) over it. Top with the remaining steak. Brush the top with 2 tablespoons of the butter, melted. Arrange the lemon slices over the steak. Bake in a preheated moderate oven (350°F.) about 35 minutes, or until fork tender. Serves 4.

Stuffing: Sauté the onions in 4 tablespoons of butter until tender. Add the mushrooms and sauté 4 minutes. Mix in the bread, parsley and milk. Season with salt and pepper.

Fish Solianka from Russia

Russians are extremely fond of a fish stew, *solianka*, which contains a number of piquant flavorings. The name derives, however, from their word for salt.

1 medium onion, chopped	*1 pound fish fillets*
3 tablespoons butter or	*2 bay leaves*
margarine	*1 cup sliced cucumbers,*
½ pound fresh mushrooms	*sprinkled with salt*
3 tablespoons tomato purée	*2 teaspoons capers, drained*
1 can (1 pound) sauerkraut,	*Garnishes: olives, lemon*
drained	*slices, chopped fresh dill*
2 teaspoons sugar	*Fine dry bread crumbs*
Salt, pepper to taste	

Sauté the onion in the butter in a saucepan until soft. Add the mushrooms and sauté for 4 minutes. Add the tomato purée, sauerkraut, sugar, salt and pepper and cook for 10 minutes. Cut the fish into pieces. Put in a saucepan with the bay leaves, cucumbers and capers. Add water to cover. Cook slowly, covered, about 12 minutes, or until the fish is tender. Spoon the mushroom mixture and fish combination, in layers, into a buttered shallow baking dish. Top with the garnishes. Sprinkle with bread crumbs. Dot with butter. Cook in a preheated moderate oven (350°F.) about 15 minutes. Serves 4.

Baked Bass with Mushroom Stuffing

Americans have a number of fresh and saltwater fish with spiny fins all of which are called bass. Most have delicate and flavorful flesh and are excellent for stuffing.

1 striped bass, about 3
    pounds (with head and
    tail removed)
Salt, pepper
1/4 cup minced green onions
1/2 cup chopped celery

2 cups chopped mushrooms,
    fresh or canned
1/2 cup butter or margarine
1 tablespoon lemon juice
2 cups soft bread cubes
1/2 teaspoon dried rosemary

Clean, wash and dry the fish. Sprinkle inside and out with salt. Sauté the onions, celery and mushrooms in the butter and lemon juice for 4 minutes. Toss with the bread cubes and rosemary. Season with salt and pepper. Spoon into the fish cavity. Close the opening with small skewers. Place in a well-greased baking dish. Bake, uncovered, in a preheated moderate oven (350°F.) about 45 minutes, or until the fish is fork tender. Serve, garnished with lemon slices if desired. Serves 4.

Rumanian Baked Fish with Vegetables

In the Balkan cuisines, favorite dishes are made by baking any local varieties of fish with well seasoned vegetable medleys. They are eaten both hot and cold.

3 or 4 pound fish, cleaned
    (head and tail removed)
Salt, pepper

3 medium tomatoes, peeled
    & cut up
1/2 teaspoon dried oregano

1 medium onion, sliced
1-2 garlic cloves, crushed
1 large carrot, diced
⅓ cup olive or salad oil
1 cup cut-up green beans

½ pound fresh whole
*   medium mushrooms*
2 tablespoons butter
1 medium lemon, sliced
3 tablespoons chopped parsley
½ cup dry white wine

Wash and dry the fish. Sprinkle inside and out with salt and pepper. Place in a buttered shallow baking dish. Sauté the onion, garlic and carrot in the oil for 5 minutes. Add the beans, tomatoes and oregano. Season with salt and pepper. Cook slowly, uncovered, for 10 minutes. Spoon over the fish. Sauté the mushrooms in the butter for 5 minutes. Spoon over the vegetable mixture. Top with the lemon slices and parsley. Pour in the wine. Cook, uncovered, in a preheated medium oven (350°F.) for 40 to 60 minutes, until the fish flesh flakes easily. Baste occasionally with the drippings while cooking. Serves 4.

Shrimp alla Cacciatore

From the Italians we have inherited a flavorful manner of cooking called *alla cacciatore,* or hunter's style. This recipe makes a good luncheon dish or an appealing buffet fare.

1 medium onion, chopped
1-2 garlic cloves, crushed
¼ cup olive oil
2 tablespoons butter or
*   margarine*
½ pound fresh mushrooms,
*   thickly sliced*
½ cup chopped green pepper
1 can (1 pound, 3 ounces)
*   tomatoes*

1 pound raw shrimp, shelled
*   & cleaned*
½ cup dry red wine
¼ teaspoon dried basil
⅛ teaspoon dried oregano
Salt, pepper to taste
3 tablespoons chopped fresh
*   parsley*

Sauté the onion and garlic in the oil and butter in a large saucepan until tender. Add the mushrooms and sauté for 3 minutes. Stir in the green pepper, tomatoes, shrimp, wine, basil, oregano, salt and pepper and cook slowly, uncovered, about 20 minutes, until the shrimp are tender. Mix in the parsley. Serve with hot cooked pasta or rice. Serves 4 to 6.

Fish Mousse with Mushroom Sauce

We acquired the culinary term *mousse* from the French. It means froth and generally refers to such rich and frothy dishes as this one.

1¼ pounds fish fillets (gray sole, salmon, halibut)	2 shallots or large green onions, minced
1 teaspoon Worcestershire sauce	½ pound fresh mushrooms, sliced
2 teaspoons grated onion	2 tablespoons flour
Salt, pepper to taste	1½ cups light cream
3 egg whites	2 tablespoons dry sherry
1 cup heavy cream	Grated nutmeg, salt, pepper
3 tablespoons butter	to taste

Cook the fillets by steaming them until just tender. Drain and cut up very finely. Mix with the Worcestershire, onion, salt and pepper. Beat the egg whites until stiff. Fold into the fish mixture. Fold in the cream. Spoon into a buttered 1 quart baking dish or mold. Set in a pan of hot water. Bake in a preheated moderate oven (375°F.) about 40 minutes, or until firm. Unmold on a warm platter. Serve with the mushroom sauce (recipe below). Serves 4.

Sauce: Melt the butter in a saucepan. Add the shallots and sauté until tender. Add the mushrooms and sauté for 4 minutes. Mix in the flour. Gradually add the cream and cook slowly, stirring, until thickened. Add the sherry, nutmeg, salt and pepper. Mix well and remove from the heat.

Deviled Clams and Mushrooms

A good brunch or luncheon dish. Serve with a green vegetable such as asparagus or broccoli.

1 pint clams
1 small onion, minced
1 garlic clove, crushed
¼ cup butter or margarine
1 cup chopped mushrooms, fresh or canned
1 tablespoon lemon juice
¼ cup chopped green pepper
2 teaspoons flour

1 tablespoon chili sauce
2 drops Tabasco or other hot sauce
Salt, pepper to taste
1 large egg, beaten
2 tablespoons chopped parsley
½ cup cracker crumbs

Drain the clams and chop them. Sauté the onion and garlic in the butter in a saucepan until tender. Add the mushrooms, lemon juice and green peper and sauté for 4 minutes. Stir in the flour. Add the clams, chili sauce and hot sauce, salt and pepper and cook slowly, stirring, until thickened. Mix a little of the hot mixture with the egg. Return to the pan. Add the parsley and cracker crumbs. Mix well and spoon into 6 buttered shells or ramekins. Dot with butter. Bake in a preheated hot oven (400°F.) about 10 minutes, or until golden on top. Serves 6.

New England Codfish Cakes with Mushrooms

Old favorites, such as codfish cakes, take on a new look when offered with an adornment of mushrooms.

2 cups flaked, cooked cod
4 cups mashed potatoes
2 eggs, slightly beaten
8 tablespoons (about) butter
1 tablespoon grated onion

Pepper to taste
1 pound fresh mushrooms,
    cleaned & sliced
2 tablespoons lemon juice
¼ cup chopped fresh parsley

Combine the cod, potatoes, eggs, 2 tablespoons of butter, grated onion and pepper. Mix well. Shape into round, flat cakes. Fry in butter until golden. Sauté the sliced mushrooms in 3 tablespoons of butter and the lemon juice for 5 minutes. Spoon over the hot codfish cakes. Serve garnished with the parsley. Serves 6.

German Fischragout

A nourishing fish stew for a winter evening meal.

1½ pounds fish fillets
    (haddock, pike, perch,
    flounder)
1 large onion, sliced
3 tablespoons butter
1 can (8 ounces) mushroom
    slices or stems and pieces,
    drained

1 tablespoon lemon juice
3 tablespoons flour
1 tablespoon drained capers
2 teaspoons chopped fresh dill
Salt, pepper to taste

Cook the fish fillets in water to cover until just tender. Drain, reserving the liquid, and cut into bite-size pieces. Sauté the onions in the butter in a saucepan until tender. Add the mushrooms and lemon juice and sauté for 3 minutes. Stir in the flour and cook 1 minute. Gradually add the reserved liquid, adding water to make 2 cups if not enough, and cook slowly, stirring, until thickened and smooth. Add the fish fillets, capers, dill, salt and pepper and leave on the stove long enough to heat through. Serves 4.

Mushroom-Seafood Coquilles

In French a *coquille* is a shell but we think of it as a flavorful dish served in a shell. This easy-to-prepare *coquille* may be served as a first course or luncheon entrée.

1 can (6½ ounces) crabmeat, cleaned	*3 tablespoons dry sherry*
	Salt, pepper to taste
1 can (about 7 ounces) minced clams	*20 large fresh mushrooms*
	3 tablespoons butter
1 can (10¾ ounces) condensed cheddar cheese soup	*Grated nutmeg*

Combine the crabmeat, clams, cheese soup, sherry, salt and pepper in a saucepan and cook over low heat for 2 minutes. Gently pull the stems from the mushrooms. Use the stems for another dish. Sauté the caps in the butter for 4 minutes. Spoon into 4 *coquille* dishes. Cover with the sauce, dividing evenly. Bake in a preheated moderate oven (375°F.) about 12 minutes. Serves 4.

French Mushroom Shrimp Flan

An open pastry shell, called a *flan* in French, can be cooked with a number of inviting fillings. This is an excellent entrée for a women's lunch.

Standard pie crust for 1-crust
   9-inch pie
½ pound fresh mushrooms
2 tablespoons butter
Freshly grated nutmeg
1 tablespoon dry sherry
1 can (10 ounces) frozen
   cream of shrimp soup

½ cup milk
⅛ teaspoon paprika
Salt and pepper
¼ pound cooked and cleaned
   small or medium shrimp
3 eggs, beaten

Line an 8-inch pie pan with the crust. Cook it according to the package directions. Clean the mushrooms and wipe dry. Cut into thick slices, reserving three caps. Melt the butter in a saucepan. Add the mushrooms and sauté for 4 minutes. Stir in the nutmeg and sherry. Remove from the heat.

Combine the soup and milk in a saucepan and heat. Add the sautéed mushrooms and drippings, the paprika, salt and pepper. Cook for 1 minute to blend the flavors. Spoon some of the hot mixture into the beaten eggs. Return to the saucepan and leave over low heat just long enough to thicken. Add the shrimp and turn into the baked pie shell. Garnish with the three reserved mushroom caps, each brushed with butter. Bake in a preheated oven (400°F.) for about 25 minutes, or until a knife inserted into the filling comes out clean. Cool slightly before serving. Cut into wedges. Serves 6.

Poultry and Game

Domesticated fowl, small game and game birds have long had universal appeal and a place of honor on the dining table. The very popular chicken, turkey, duckling and Rock Cornish hen, as well as the lesser known rabbit, quail, goose and partridge, among others, all combine with mushrooms to make inviting culinary creations.

In ancient Egypt two of the earliest types of poultry, chicken and ducks, which had migrated from Southwest Asia, were, like mushrooms, regarded as "foods for the Gods." The banquets of the early Greeks featured platters of "poultry, ducks, pigeons, and a goose" as a first course. For the gargantuan Roman feasts the different kinds of fowl were baked in pies, stuffed with flavorful grain combinations and prepared with sauces of various ingredients.

Other Europeans became devotees of poultry and game but it was Henry IV of France who did much to popularize the chicken with his famous pronouncement, "I want there to be no peasant in my kingdom so poor that he is unable to have a chicken in his pot every Sunday."

Inventive cooks in Europe and the Orient devised many a superb dish combining poultry and game with mushrooms, of both the cultivated and wild varieties. A number of these inviting creations were adapted and adopted in America, but we have also created some superlative similar dishes of our own.

Unfortunately, early Americans were not always sure of the quality of their fowl unless it was raised in their own back yards.

Travellers, for example, complained that some tavern cooks served poultry "before the life had been an hour out of their bodies." As time progressed, our poultry was greatly improved and served more frequently.

By the early 1800's recipes for chicken pie, a most popular dish, also included mushrooms. In 1829 a recipe for chicken *au soleil* listed among the ingredients, "a handful of buttered mushrooms." By the late 19th century such a fashionable restaurant as Delmonico's in New York featured elegant poultry and mushroom creations, including capons garnished with fluted mushrooms and chicken breast dishes such as *à la Certosa*, *à la Volnay* and *à la Beranger*.

Our grandparents took great pride in serving chicken for company dinners, particularly on Sunday, and turkey was featured at holiday get-togethers. Today we have excellent poultry and game which is readily available the year round and is served for family meals as well as for entertaining. They are featured at meals served both indoors and out.

This selection includes some of the better known international dishes as well as American poultry and game creations, all enriched by the addition of mushrooms.

Mushroom-Stuffed Rock Cornish Hens

An elegant main course for a holiday meal. Serve with a rice dish.

3 frozen Rock Cornish hens
  (about 1 pound each)
Salt, pepper to taste
Juice of 1 large lemon
½ cup minced green onions
Butter (about ¼ cup)

2¼ cups sautéed fresh
  mushrooms
Grated fresh nutmeg to taste
3 tablespoons chopped fresh
  parsley
1 tablespoon cornstarch
2 cups grapefruit juice

Thaw the hens. Wash them and wipe dry. Sprinkle inside and out with salt and pepper. Sprinkle the skin with lemon juice and rub with the fingers. Sauté the onions in 2 tablespoons of butter until tender. Mix with the mushrooms, nutmeg and parsley. Season with salt and pepper. Spoon into the cavities. Tie the legs. Brush each hen with melted butter. Put in a shallow baking dish. Roast in a preheated hot oven (425°F.) about 1¼ hours, until tender. Baste with the drippings while cooking. Remove to a plate and keep warm. Scrape the drippings in the pan. Mix the cornstarch and grapefruit juice. Add to the pan and cook slowly, stirring, until thickened. Strain and pour into a gravy dish to be served with the hens at the table. Untie the legs and split each hen in half before serving. Serves 6.

Coq au Vin Rouge

The French dish of chicken cooked in wine with small white onions and mushrooms has become most popular in America. There are several ways of preparing it. This is but one of them.

*1 frying chicken, about 3
  pounds, cut-up*
Salt, pepper to taste
5 tablespoons butter
*2 tablespoons (about) olive
  oil*
*1 small piece lean bacon,
  diced*
*1½ pounds small white
  onions, peeled*
*¾ pound medium, fresh
  mushrooms*
¼ cup brandy
2 cups dry red wine
¼ teaspoon dried thyme
1 bay leaf
2 sprigs parsley
2 garlic cloves, crushed
2 tablespoons flour
*3 tablespoons chopped fresh
  parsley*

Wash the chicken pieces and wipe dry. Season with salt and

pepper. Heat 3 tablespoons of the butter, oil and bacon in a large heavy kettle or casserole. Add the onions and sauté about 10 minutes, depending on the size. (Cook a little less time if very small.) Remove the onions with a slotted spoon and set aside. Add the mushrooms to the drippings and sauté 5 minutes, adding more oil if necessary. Remove and set aside. Add the chicken pieces to the drippings and fry until golden on all sides. Pour in the brandy and ignite it. Let burn, shaking the pan, until the flames subside. Return the onions to the kettle. Add the wine, thyme, bay leaf, parsley sprigs and garlic. Season with salt and pepper. Bring to a boil. Lower the heat and cook slowly, covered, about 30 minutes, or until the chicken is tender. Add the mushrooms during the last 5 minutes of cooking. Blend together 2 tablespoons of softened butter and the flour. Add to the liquid and stir with a whisk until well blended. Arrange the chicken, onions and mushrooms on a platter. Cover with the sauce. Garnish with the parsley. Serves 4 to 6.

Balkan Baked Duckling with Sauerkraut and Mushrooms

A most flavorful dish for a winter dinner party.

6 dried mushrooms	2 tablespoons paprika
1 duckling, 4 to 5 pounds	2 pounds sauerkraut, drained
Salt, pepper to taste	1 cup chopped green peppers
2 large onions, chopped	½ teaspoon dried thyme
2 tablespoons fat (bacon drippings or lard)	1½ cups tomato juice

Soak the mushrooms in lukewarm water to cover for 20 minutes. Drain, pressing to release all the liquid. Slice mushrooms and reserve the liquid. Wash the duckling and wipe dry.

Sprinkle with salt and pepper. Prick the skin in several places. Place in a roasting pan and cook in a preheated slow oven (325°F.) for 1½ hours.

While the duckling is cooking, sauté the onions in the fat in a saucepan. Add the paprika and cook 1 minute. Stir in the sauerkraut, sliced mushrooms, peppers and thyme. Pour in the reserved mushroom liquid and tomato juice. Season with salt and pepper. Cook slowly, covered, for 30 minutes.

When the duckling has cooked, take from the oven. Remove to a platter. Spoon off all except 2 tablespoons of the fat. Add the sauerkraut mixture to the pan and mix with the drippings. Place the duckling over the sauerkraut. Return to the oven and cook another 30 to 45 minutes, until the duckling is tender. Cut up and serve surrounded with the sauerkraut mixture. Serves 4 to 6.

Poularde Basque

The Basque region of northwest Spain and southwest France is famous for its good cooking. Fine ingredients typical of the area are used in this chicken dish.

1 roasting chicken, about 4 pounds
Salt, pepper to taste
½ teaspoon dried rosemary
3 tablespoons butter
2 sprigs parsley
Olive oil
1 large onion, sliced
2 garlic cloves, crushed
1 medium eggplant, unpeeled & cubed
3 medium tomatoes, peeled & chopped
1 cup chicken broth
1 bay leaf
½ teaspoon dried thyme
3 sprigs parsley
2 medium green peppers, cleaned & sliced
½ pound whole medium fresh mushrooms, cleaned & dried

Wash the chicken and wipe dry. Season with salt and pepper. Place the rosemary, 1 tablespoon of butter and parsley in the cavity. Tie the legs. Heat 2 tablespoons of butter and ¼ cup of olive oil in a large heavy casserole or kettle. Add the chicken, breast side down, and fry until golden, turning carefully with two spoons to brown on all sides. Remove the chicken. Add the onions and garlic and sauté until tender. Add the eggplant cubes, and more oil, as needed, and fry until tender. Add the tomatoes and cook 1 minute. Return the chicken to the kettle. Add the broth, bay leaf, thyme and parsley. Season with salt and pepper. Bring to a boil. Lower the heat and cook slowly, covered, for about 1¼ hours, until the chiken is tender. Add the peppers and mushrooms during the last 10 minutes of cooking. Untie the legs and discard the parsley. Serve the chicken surrounded with the vegetables. Serves 4 to 6.

Summer Turkey-Mushroom Loaf

An excellent and attractive dish for an outdoor luncheon or buffet. The loaf can easily be prepared beforehand and kept ready in the refrigerator.

¼ cup vinegar or lemon juice
⅓ cup salad oil
½ teaspoon paprika
Salt, pepper to taste
1½ cups sliced raw mushrooms
2 cups diced cooked turkey
2 tablespoons unflavored gelatine
½ cup cold water
2½ cups hot turkey or chicken broth
2 hard-cooked eggs, sliced
½ cup cooked peas
6 small mushroom caps
½ cup chopped green pepper

Combine the vinegar, oil, paprika, salt and pepper. Pour

over the mushrooms and turkey in a large bowl. Leave for 1 hour, stirring occasionally. Soak the gelatine in the cold water. Add to the hot broth and dissolve. Let cool. Arrange the egg slices, peas and mushrooms on the bottom of a loaf pan or mold to make a decorative pattern. Pour ½ cup of the cooled broth and gelatine to form a thin layer over them. Chill in the refrigerator until firm. Combine the remaining thickened broth with the turkey-mushroom mixture. Mix in the green pepper. Spoon into the pan over the chilled ingredients. Chill until firm. Unmold on a cold platter. Serves 6 to 8.

Chicken-Mushroom Kebabs Indienne

These kebabs are good fare for an outdoor luncheon or or supper.

4 whole chicken breasts	¼ teaspoon chili powder
1 cup plain yogurt	Salt, pepper to taste
2 tablespoons lemon juice	40 small whole fresh
½ teaspoon turmeric powder	mushrooms, cleaned
½ teaspoon ground ginger	20 pieces green pepper
⅛ teaspoon ground cumin	

Remove the skin from the chicken breasts. Cut off the meat and discard the bones. Cut the chicken into 1½ inch cubes and place into a large bowl. Add the yogurt, lemon juice, turmeric, ginger, cumin, chili, salt, pepper, and mushrooms. Mix well. Leave to marinate 1 to 2 hours. Thread a chicken cube, mushroom and piece of green pepper alternately on small skewers until all the ingredients are used. Brush with the marinade. Cook on an outdoor grill or under an oven broiler, turning once, until the chicken is tender. Serves 4 to 6.

Southern Smothered Chicken and Mushrooms

2 frying chickens, about 2½   1½ cups hot chicken broth
    pounds each, quartered   1 pound fresh mushrooms
Paprika, salt, pepper to taste   1 cup light cream
½ cup butter or margarine

Wash the chicken pieces and wipe dry. Sprinkle with paprika, salt and pepper. Melt the butter in a skillet. Add the chicken
and sauté, turning, until golden on all sides. Remove to a baking
dish. Add the chicken broth. Bake, covered, in a preheated moderate oven (350°F.) for 1 hour. Baste occasionally while cooking.

Clean the mushrooms and wipe dry. Pull the stems from
the caps. Set aside the stems to use for another dish. When the
chicken has cooked 1 hour, add the mushroom caps and cream
to it and cook about 10 minutes longer, or until the chicken is
tender. Serve the chicken covered with the mushrooms and
sauce. Serves 6 to 8.

Breakfast Braised Quail and Mushrooms

4 quail, cleaned   1½ cups dry white wine
½ cup (about) butter   ½ teaspoon dried rosemary
1 pound fresh mushrooms,   Salt, pepper to taste
    thickly sliced   4 rounds buttered white bread

Brown the quail on all sides in the butter in a large skillet.
With a slotted spoon remove quail to a warm platter. Add the
mushrooms to the drippings, adding more butter if needed, and
sauté for 4 minutes. Remove and set aside. Return the quail to

the skillet. Add the wine, rosemary, salt and pepper and cook slowly, covered, about 30 minutes, or until tender. Return the mushrooms to the skillet 5 minutes before the cooking is finished. Remove the quail and mushrooms to a warm platter. Fry the rounds of bread in the warm drippings. Serve each quail over a fried round of bread. Spoon any remaining gravy over the quail. Serves 4.

Chicken Livers and Mushrooms Smetana

This easy-to-prepare dish may be elegantly served from a chafing dish for a late evening repast.

1 pound chicken livers	¼ cup white wine
3 tablespoons flour	1 can (8 ounces) sliced
Paprika, salt, pepper to taste	mushrooms, drained
¼ cup butter or margarine	1 cup sour cream, at room
½ cup chicken broth	temperature

Dredge the chicken livers with the flour, seasoned with paprika, salt and pepper. Melt the butter in a skillet. Add the chicken livers and sauté for 4 minutes. Stir in the broth, wine and mushrooms, and cook slowly about 3 minutes. Mix in the sour cream and leave on the stove just long enough to heat through. Serve over toast points. Serves 4.

Impromptu Chicken Casserole

Everyone is occasionally faced with the necessity of producing a meal in a hurry with ingredients from the kitchen shelf. This casserole is for just such an event. Use canned chicken, if desired.

¼ cup finely chopped onion
¼ cup chopped green pepper
3 tablespoons butter or
    margarine
1 can (10½ ounces)
    condensed cream of
    celery soup
1 cup sour cream

1 jar (about 4½ ounces)
    whole mushrooms,
    drained
2 cups diced cooked chicken
3 cups cooked pasta (maca-
    roni, noodles or
    spaghetti)
Grated Parmesan cheese

Sauté the onion and green pepper in the butter until tender. Remove from the heat and combine with the remaining ingredients except the cheese. Turn into a buttered 2-quart casserole. Sprinkle with the cheese. Bake in a preheated moderate oven (350°F.) for 30 minutes. Serves 6.

Pollo alla Cacciatora

This hunter's dish from Italy is a favorite for any dinner.

2 frying chickens, about 2½
    pounds each, cut-up
Salt, pepper to taste
¼ cup butter or margarine

2 medium onions, sliced
1-2 garlic cloves, crushed
1 can (1 pound 12 ounces)
    Italian style tomatoes

3 tablespoons (about) olive
 oil
¾ pound fresh mushrooms,
 cleaned & sliced

1 cup dry white wine
½ teaspoon dried thyme
½ teaspoon dried oregano
¼ cup chopped fresh parsley

Wash the chicken pieces and wipe dry. Season with salt and pepper. Heat the butter and oil in a large kettle. Add the chicken and brown on all sides until golden. Remove to a plate. Add the mushrooms to the drippings and sauté for 4 minutes. With a slotted spoon, remove to a plate. Add the onions and garlic and more oil, if needed. Sauté until the onions are tender. Return the chicken pieces to the kettle. Add the tomatoes, wine, thyme, oregano and season with salt and pepper. Bring to a boil. Lower the heat and cook slowly, covered, about 45 minutes, or until the chicken is tender. Stir in the mushrooms and parsley 5 minutes before the cooking is finished. Serves 8.

Suprèmes de Volaille aux Champignons

The skinless and boneless raw breast of chicken, called in French suprème de volaille, is a great delicacy. It must be cooked briefly and with special attention so that each suprème is tender and juicy.

4 half chicken breasts
Salt, white pepper to taste
Juice of 1 large lemon
¼ cup butter
1 small onion, minced

1½ cups sliced mushrooms,
 fresh or canned
¼ cup chicken bouillon
¼ cup dry white wine
1 cup heavy cream

Pull off the skin from each of the chicken breasts. Loosen the flesh from the bone. Pull out the bone and pieces of cartilage. Cut the meat away from the bones. Pull out the white tendon.

Sprinkle the chicken with salt, pepper and 1 tablespoon of lemon juice. Melt the butter in a skillet and sauté the chicken in it for 6 to 8 minutes, until white or, if pressed with the finger, soft but springy. Do not overcook. Remove from the heat and keep warm.

Add the onion and mushrooms to the drippings and sauté for 4 minutes. Season with salt and pepper. Add the bouillon and wine and cook over high heat until glossy. Stir in the cream and cook until the mixture thickens slightly. Season with salt, pepper and the remaining lemon juice. Pour over the chicken and serve. Serves 4.

Japanese Chicken-Mushroom Yakitori

In Japan foods that are grilled are termed *yakitori*. Very often they are cooked on small *hibachis* for outdoor meals.

2 *whole chicken breasts*
1 *pound chicken livers,*
    washed
24 *small whole mushrooms,*
    cleaned & dried
⅓ *cup soy sauce*

⅓ *cup sake or dry sherry*
1 *tablespoon sugar*
⅓ *cup peanut oil*
2 *teaspoons minced ginger*
    root
Pepper

Remove the skin and bones of the chicken and cut into 1-inch cubes. Cut the livers into cubes of the same size. Put in a bowl with the mushrooms. Cover with the soy sauce, *sake*, sugar, oil and ginger root. Season with pepper. Leave to marinate for 2 hours. String the chicken cubes, livers and mushrooms alternately on small skewers. Grill over hot coals or under a broiler, turning once, until tender, about 10 minutes. Serves about 6.

NOTE: If the marinade is not sufficient, make more. The exact amount required will depend on the weight of the chicken.

Roast Chicken with Mushroom-Rice Stuffing

For a change of pace, try this unusual stuffing for roast chicken.

1 roasting chicken (3½ to 4 pounds)	2 cups sliced mushrooms, fresh or canned
Salt, pepper to taste	½ cup uncooked rice
3 tablespoons minced onion	½ teaspoon curry powder
4 tablespoons butter	2 tablespoons chopped fresh parsley

Wash and dry the chicken. Sprinkle the inside with salt and pepper. Sauté the onion in 2 tablespoons of butter until tender. Add the mushrooms and sauté for 2 minutes. Stir in the rice, curry powder and parsley. Season with salt and pepper. Stuff the chicken with the mixture. Tie the legs. Place in a baking pan. Brush the skin with 2 tablespoons of melted butter. Sprinkle with salt and pepper. Cover with a piece of foil. Roast in a preheated slow oven (325°F.) for about 2 hours, or until the chicken is tender. Remove the foil for the last 45 minutes of cooking. Serves 4 to 6.

Chinese Walnut Chicken with Mushrooms

Serve this dish with some other Chinese dishes for a buffet or by itself as a light entrée for a supper or luncheon.

6 Chinese dried black   1 tablespoon cornstarch
      mushrooms   3 tablespoons soy sauce
6 green onions, sliced   1 teaspoon sugar
¼ cup peanut oil   1 cup chicken bouillon
2 cups* raw breast of chicken, 1 large green pepper, chopped
      cut into thin slices   1 cup chopped walnuts

Soak the mushrooms in lukewarm water to cover for 20 minutes. Drain, pressing to release all the liquid. Slice. Sauté the onions in the oil until tender. Add the chicken and mushrooms and fry until the chicken is tender. Combine the cornstarch, soy sauce and sugar and add, with the bouillon, to the chicken mixture. Cook, stirring, until thickened. Mix in the green pepper and walnuts and cook about 5 minutes. Serves 4.

*The meat from about 4 half chicken breasts.

Continental Chicken-Mushroom Hash

An excellent brunch or luncheon dish that can be prepared beforehand and cooked after guests arrive.

1 large onion, chopped   Salt, white pepper to taste
¼ cup minced shallots or   3 cups diced cooked chicken
      green onions   ½ pound sliced fresh
¼ cup butter   mushrooms, previously
2 tablespoons flour   sautéed in butter
1 cup light cream   Fine dry bread crumbs
½ cup dry white wine   Grated Parmesan cheese

Sauté the onion and shallots in the butter in a large saucepan until tender. Stir in the flour. Gradually add the cream and wine. Cook slowly, stirring, until thickened. Add the salt, pepper,

chicken and mushrooms. Spoon into a buttered shallow baking
dish. Sprinkle with bread crumbs and grated cheese. Dot with
butter. Bake on the top shelf of a preheated hot oven (425°F.)
about 20 minutes, until golden to top. Serves 6.

German King's Patty Shells

Germans are devoted to their *Königinpastetchen*, which are
patty shells filled with a mixture of chicken, tongue and mushrooms in a flavorful wine sauce. A good luncheon dish.

⅓ cup diced cooked tongue   1 cup chicken bouillon
2 cups sliced mushrooms,   ¼ cup dry white wine
   fresh or canned   2 cups diced cooked chicken
4 tablespoons butter   Salt, pepper to taste
2 teaspoons lemon juice   2 egg yolks
2 tablespoons flour   6 hot patty shells

Sauté the tongue and mushrooms in the butter and lemon
juice in a saucepan for 4 minutes. Stir in the flour. Gradually
add the bouillon and wine and cook slowly, stirring, until
thickened. Add the chicken, salt and pepper. Beat the egg yolks
until creamy. Stir some of the hot mixture with it. Return to
the chicken mixture and stir well. Spoon into the hot patty shells.
Serves 6.

Partridges in Mushroom Sauce

Plump and pleasing partridges, either fresh or frozen, gain
additional appeal when cooked with flavorings of wine, juniper
berries, sour cream and mushrooms.

4 partridges, dressed
Salt, pepper to taste
4 slices bacon
1 cup chopped onions
3 tablespoons butter
½ pound fresh mushrooms,
    sliced
½ cup dry white wine

1 cup meat bouillon
4 dried juniper berries,
    crushed (available in
    spice departments)
Salt, pepper to taste
½ cup sour cream, at room
    temperature

Sprinkle each partridge with salt and pepper and wrap with a slice of bacon. Place in a large heavy casserole. Sauté the onions in the butter in a small skillet until tender. Add the mushrooms and sauté for 4 minutes. Spoon over the partridges. Add the wine, bouillon and juniper berries. Season with salt and pepper. Bake, covered, in a preheated moderate oven (325°F.) for 1 to 1½ hours, until tender. When cooked, remove the partridges to a platter and keep warm. Spoon the onions and mushrooms over them. Pour the liquid into a saucepan and bring to a boil. Lower the heat and add the sour cream. When heated, pour over the partridges. Serves 4.

Japanese Chicken and Vegetables

In the Japanese cuisine each type of cookery has a specific name. Boiled foods, for example, are called *nimono*. Generally the dish includes the mushrooms known as *shiitake*.

4 shiitake or other Oriental
    dried mushrooms
4 cups sliced uncooked
    chicken
Chicken broth
Sugar to taste

1 package (6 ounces) frozen
    green pea pods (snow
    peas)
2 medium carrots, diced
1 teaspoon monosodium
    glutanate

Sake or dry sherry to taste   ½ cup sliced bamboo shoots
                               2 tablespoons soy sauce

Soak the *shiitake* in lukewarm water to cover for 20 minutes. Drain, pressing to release all the liquid. Slice. Cook the chicken in broth to cover which is flavored with sugar and *sake* until the flesh is tender; drain. Cook the snow peas and carrots also in broth flavored with sugar and *sake*; drain. Combine the mushrooms, chicken and vegetables with the bamboo shoots in a saucepan. Add the monosodium glutamate, 1 teaspoon sugar, soy sauce and chicken broth to cover and cook a few minutes. Serves 4.

Chicken Breasts Riviera

This colorful dish is ingeniously flavored with favorite foods from the lovely southern coast of France.

6 half chicken breasts   ¼ cup tomato paste
Salt, pepper to taste   1 cup hot water
⅓ cup olive oil   1 cup dry white wine
2 tablespoons butter or   ½ teaspoon dried rosemary
   margarine   2 cups sliced fresh mushrooms
2 medium onions, sliced   2 tablespoons chopped fresh
2 garlic cloves, crushed   herbs

Remove and discard the skin from each chicken breast. Wash and wipe dry. Sprinkle with salt and pepper. Heat the oil and butter in a large skillet. Add the chicken breasts and fry until golden on both sides. Remove to a plate. Add the onions and garlic to the drippings and sauté until tender. Stir in the tomato paste. Add the water, wine and rosemary. Season with salt and pepper. Bring to a boil. Lower the heat and return the chicken breasts to the skillet. Cook slowly, covered, about 30 minutes, or until tender. Add the mushrooms 10 minutes before the cooking is finished. Stir in fresh herbs. Serves 6.

Napoleon's Poulet Marengo

This well known chicken dish was created by Napoleon's chef, Dunand, after the French had won a great victory against the Austrians in the north Italian town of Marengo in 1800. There were practically no provisions available but scouts found a scrawny chicken, three eggs, four tomatoes and six crayfish with which the celebration feast was prepared. Wine and mushrooms were later additions.

2 frying chickens, about 2½
    pounds each, cut-up
Salt, pepper to taste
6 tablespoons olive oil
3 tablespoons butter
1 pound fresh mushrooms,
    cleaned & dried
2 garlic cloves
1 cup chopped onions
⅓ cup tomato purée
1 cup dry white wine

4 medium tomatoes, peeled,
    seeded, chopped
1 bouquet garni (bay leaf,
    parsley, thyme)
Garnishes: 8 eggs, deep fried
    in olive oil; 4 slices
    French bread, fried in oil
    & cut into triangles; 16
    cooked, shelled deveined
    large shrimp

Wash the chicken pieces and wipe dry. Season with salt and pepper. Heat the oil and butter in a large heavy casserole or frying pan. Add the chicken pieces and fry until golden on all sides. Remove to a warm platter. Carefully pull the stems from half the mushrooms. Reserve the caps. Slice the stems and the other half pound of mushrooms. Sauté in the drippings for

4 minutes. With a slotted spoon, remove to a plate. Add the garlic and onions to the drippings and sauté until tender. Stir in the tomato purée and wine. Bring to a boil. Cook over high heat for 5 minutes. Return the chicken pieces to the kettle. Add the tomatoes, *bouquet garni*, salt and pepper. Cook slowly, covered, for about 35 minutes, until the chicken is tender. Add the reserved sautéed sliced mushrooms and mushroom caps 10 minutes before the cooking is finished. Remove and discard the *bouquet garni*. To serve, arrange the chicken pieces on a large platter. Spoon the tomato sauce and sliced mushrooms over them. Top with the mushroom caps. Arrange the fried eggs, each on a toast triangle, and the shrimp around the chicken.   Serves 8.

Poulet Sauté aux Champignons

A good dinner dish which can be easily prepared.

6 half chicken breasts	¼ cup white wine or water
Salt, pepper to taste	½ teaspoon dried rosemary
3 tablespoons butter	24 small or medium, fresh
2 tablespoons salad oil	mushroom caps
1 can (10½ ounces)	2 tablespoons lemon juice
condensed cream of	2 tablespoons dry sherry
mushroom soup	

Remove the skin from each chicken breast. Season with salt and pepper. Heat the butter and oil in a large skillet. Add the chicken and sauté for 5 minutes. Add the soup, wine and rosemary. Season with salt and pepper. Cook slowly, covered, for 20 minutes. Add the mushroom caps, sprinkled with the lemon juice, and cook another 10 minutes. Stir in the sherry. Serves 6.

Luncheon Turkey Mushroom Salad

Excellent for a women's get-together. Serve with buttered hot rolls and herb-flavored stewed tomatoes.

2 cups sliced fresh mushrooms
2 cups diced cooked turkey
1 cup sliced celery
3/4 cup French dressing
1 cup cooked green peas
1/2 cup sour cream
1/4 cup almond slivers
Salt, pepper to taste
Lettuce leaves

Marinate mushrooms, turkey and celery in French dressing for 1 hour. Mix with peas, sour cream and almonds. Season with salt and pepper. Chill. Serve on lettuce leaves. Serves 4.

Central European Chicken Paprika with Mushrooms

Favorite fare in Austria and Hungary is paprika-flavored chicken to which sour cream is added. Mushrooms add further appeal to this superb dish.

2 frying chickens, about 2½
    pounds each, cut-up
Salt, pepper to taste
6 tablespoons cooking fat
2 large onions, sliced
2 tablespoons paprika
1½ cups chicken broth
1 pound fresh mushrooms,
    sliced thickly
2 medium green peppers,
    cleaned and sliced
1 tablespoon flour
1½ cups sour cream, at room
    temperature

Wash and dry the chicken. Season with salt and pepper.

Heat the fat in a large frying pan. Add the onions and sauté until tender. Stir in the paprika and cook 1 minute. Add the chicken pieces and fry on all sides until golden. Add the chicken broth and cook slowly, covered, for 45 minutes. Add the mushrooms and peppers and cook about 15 minutes longer, until the chicken is tender. Mix the flour with the sour cream and stir into the chicken mixture. Leave on the stove long enough to heat through. Serve with hot noodles. Serves 8.

Rabbit à la Provençale

In southern France there are many superb dishes made with rabbit. Our supermarkets have excellent frozen rabbit which can be used to make this flavorful combination.

1 rabbit, about 3 pounds, cut up	1 bay leaf
Salt, pepper to taste	½ teaspoon dried thyme
⅓ cup (about) oilve oil	Dry red wine
3 tablespoons butter	Salt, pepper to taste
20 small white onions, peeled	½ pound whole fresh mushrooms
2 garlic cloves, crushed	3 tablespoons chopped fresh parsley
2 large tomatoes, peeled & chopped	

Wash the rabbit pieces and wipe dry. Season with salt and pepper. Heat the oil and butter in a kettle. Add the rabbit pieces and fry on all sides until golden. Remove to a plate. Add the onions and garlic to the drippings. Add more oil, if necessary. Sauté until golden. Return the rabbit pieces to the kettle. Stir in the tomatoes, bay leaf, thyme, wine to cover, salt and pepper. Cook slowly, covered, about 30 minutes or until the rabbit is tender. Add the mushrooms 10 minutes before the dish is finished. Stir in the parsley. Serves 4.

Meats

Among the gastronomic delights that grace our tables, meats are the most treasured and are very often the stars of family and company repasts. Fortunately, we have a vast repertoire of delectable meat dishes to which mushrooms add special interest and appeal.

Since the beginning of time man has been preoccupied with obtaining meat for his daily meals. At first he was limited to the hunting of wild animals, but with the birth of civilization the flesh of domesticated cows, pigs and sheep also became available.

For centuries, however, the term "meat" was applied to any number of foods including fish, poultry, vegetables and nuts, as well as to the flesh of animals. In 1624, the English philosopher Francis Bacon commented that mushrooms "yield so delicious a meat." In modern times we have adopted the practice of using the term primarily for the flesh of our domesticated animals. That of wild animals is called game.

Early dishes of both meat and game were stews of various ingredients, cooked slowly with seasonings. The long cooking process tenderized the tough flesh and the spices acted as important preservatives. Mushrooms were added to some of these early preparations to lend flavor and enchantment.

In medieval Europe meals were gargantuan feasts, very often emphasizing meat specialties. Enormous roasts were great favorites, but large meat pies, baked dishes and stews, which had sauces, herbs and mushrooms added, were also popular preparations. Later, the dishes became more refined but they still included the flavorful fungi. A 17th century recipe for Scotch escallops instructed that the veal be flavored with "1 cup of fried mushrooms." Queen Victoria's beloved mutton cutlets included "2 ounces of minced mushrooms."

Europeans are still devotees of meat dishes flavored with mushrooms. The English enjoy their steak and kidney pie with the addition of mushrooms and very often serve them with bacon and sausage for breakfast. In Germany, mushrooms are cooked in veal and pork dishes, as well as with venison. The Scandinavians include their wild and cultivated mushrooms in rich pork and game creations, whereas in France there are such culinary classics as *blanquette de veau*, *boeuf à la bourguignonne* and various *ragoûts* which feature mushrooms. Other meat and mushroom dishes include the interesting stews of Central Europe.

In the Orient, mushrooms have been added to the favorite hot pots and national dishes such as the Japanese *sukiyaki*. We Americans have adapted many of the foreign specialties, but we also enhance the flavor of our hamburgers, meat loaves and casseroles with mushrooms and serve them as garnishes or accompaniments to our great roasts and steaks.

This selection includes some of the best of the cosmopolitan collection of marvelous meat dishes which were created by cooks over the centuries.

English Steak and Kidney Pie with Mushrooms

This favorite English dish is excellent for brunch or supper.

1 beef kidney	3 cups beef bouillon
1½ pounds round steak, cut into 1-inch cubes	½ pound fresh mushrooms, sliced
⅓ cup flour	2 tablespoons dry sherry

Salt, pepper to taste
¼ cup butter or margarine
1 small onion, minced

Standard pastry for a 1-crust
9-inch pie, unbaked
1 egg, beaten

Remove the outer membrane of the kidney. Split open and remove any fat or white veins. Cut into 1-inch pieces. Soak in salted cold water to cover for 30 minutes. Drain and wipe dry. Dredge the kidney and steak cubes with the flour, seasoned with salt and pepper. Melt the butter in a large saucepan. Add the onion and sauté until tender. Push aside. Add the dredged meats and brown. Season with salt and pepper. Add the bouillon and stir until thickened. Cook slowly, covered, about 1 hour, until the meat is tender. Add the mushrooms and sherry. Turn into a 2 quart casserole. Roll out the pastry to fit the top and place over the dish. Flute the edges and brush with beaten egg. Bake in a preheated hot oven (450°F.) for about 20 minutes, until the top is golden. Serves 6.

Continental Veal Chops with Wild Mushrooms

Canned wild mushrooms imported from Europe are expensive but great gastronomic treasures.

6 loin veal chops, about ¾
    inch thick
¼ cup cooking oil
1 medium onion, chopped
1 garlic clove, crushed
1 cup (about) dry white wine
1 teaspoon dried basil

Salt, pepper to taste
1 can (10 ounces) cèpes or
    1 can (4 ounces)
    chanterelles, drained &
    sliced
2 tablespoons (about) butter
    or margarine

Brown the chops in the oil in a large skillet. Remove to a plate. Add the onion and garlic to the drippings and sauté until tender. Return 'the chops to the pan. Pour the wine over them. Add the basil and season with salt and pepper. Cook slowly, covered, for 1 hour, or until the chops are tender. Add more wine while cooking, if needed. When the chops are almost cooked, sauté the *cèpes* or *chanterelles* in butter, (using more butter for *cèpes* than *chanterelles*) for 4 minutes. Add to the chops shortly before they have finished cooking. Serves 6.

Mushroom Meatballs Parisienne

An elegant recipe for a year-round favorite.

⅓ *cup minced green onions, with tops*

5 *tablespoons (about) butter or margarine*

2 *cups chopped mushrooms, fresh or canned*

4 *slices stale white bread*

3 *pounds ground beef*

3 *eggs, beaten slightly*

½ *cup chopped fresh parsley*

Salt, pepper to taste

2 *tablespoons flour*

2 *cups dry red wine*

Sauté the green onions in 3 tablespoons of butter until tender. Add the mushrooms and sauté 4 minutes. Spoon into a large bowl. Soak the bread in water to cover and squeeze dry. Crumble and add to the onions and mushrooms. Add the beef, eggs, parsley, salt and pepper; mix well. Shape into 2-inch balls. Brown in butter in a large skillet. Stir in the flour and add the wine. Cook slowly, covered, about 25 minutes, until the meatballs are done. Stir occasionally while cooking. Serves 10.

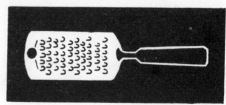

New Zealand Lamb Stew with Mushrooms

The superb New Zealand lamb exported to countries around the world is combined with vegetables in this dish to make an appealing combination for a winter dinner.

4 pounds (about) lamb
   shoulder, cut into large
   pieces
Cooking oil
2 medium onions, sliced
1 garlic clove, crushed
   (optional)
3 medium carrots, diced
2 cups dry red wine

1 teaspoon dried oregano or
   rosemary
Salt, pepper to taste
1 package (10 ounces) frozen
   green peas
½ pound sliced fresh
   mushrooms or 1 can (6
   ounces) sliced
   mushrooms, drained

Brown the meat in oil on all sides in a large kettle. Remove to a platter. Pour off any excess fat. Add the onions, garlic, carrots and more oil to the kettle. Sauté 5 minutes. Return the lamb to the kettle. Add the wine, oregano, salt and pepper. Bring to a boil. Lower the heat and cook slowly, covered, about 1¼ hours, or until the lamb is cooked. Add the peas and mushrooms 10 minutes before the cooking is finished. Serve with hot rice. Serves 6.

Russian Beef Stroganoff

This dish, which has become very popular in America, was named for a Russian gourmet and bon vivant of the Tsarist Court, Count Paul Stroganoff.

2 *pounds beef sirloin*
5 *tablespoons (about) butter*
   or margine
1 *medium onion, chopped*
½ *pound fresh mushrooms,*
   sliced
3 *tablespoons tomato paste*

1 *tablespoon prepared*
   mustard
1 *cup beef bouillon*
Pinch sugar
Salt, pepper to taste
2 *teaspoons flour*
1 *cup sour cream, at room*
   temperature

Remove any fat from the meat and cut crosswise into strips about ½ inch thick and 3 inches long. Heat 2 tablespoons of butter in a skillet. Add some of the meat and brown quickly. Remove to a plate. Add more butter and meat and brown. Remove also to a plate. Sauté the onion in the drippings. Add the mushrooms and more butter, if needed, and sauté 4 minutes. Stir in the tomato paste and mustard. Add the bouillon, sugar, salt and pepper. Bring to a boil. Lower the heat and cook slowly, covered, for 10 minutes. Add the meat and cook 5 minutes longer. Combine the flour and sour cream and add to the gravy. Leave on the stove just long enough to heat through. Serves 4.

Jambon et Champignons à la Crème

Ham and mushrooms with a cream sauce are superb for a late breakfast or brunch.

1 *medium onion, chopped*
¼ *cup butter*
1 *tablespoon lemon juice*
½ *pound fresh mushrooms,*
   sliced
¼ *cup flour*
1¾ *cups light cream*

¼ *cup tomato juice*
Freshly grated nutmeg, salt,
   pepper to taste
1 *pound thinly sliced cooked*
   ham, cut into 2-inch
   strips

Sauté the onion in the butter until tender. Add the lemon juice and mushrooms and sauté 4 minutes. Stir in the flour. Gradually add the cream and cook, stirring, until thickened. Add the tomato juice, nutmeg, salt and pepper, and cook another minute or so. Fry the ham slices in a skillet. Pour the sauce over them and put under a broiler just long enough to glaze. Serves 4.

Ragoût de Boeuf Bordelaise

This French stew, prepared "in the style of Bordeaux", is flavored with red wine, onions and mushrooms.

3 pounds beef chuck, cut into
    2-inch cubes
Flour
Salt, pepper to taste
1/4 cup cooking oil
3/4 cup minced green onions,
    with tops
1 large garlic clove, crushed
2 cups (about) red Bordeaux
    wine

2 parsley sprigs
1 small bay leaf
1/2 teaspoon dried thyme
1/2 pound fresh mushrooms,
    sliced lengthwise into
    halves
1 can (1 pound) small white
    onions, drained

Dredge the meat with flour, seasoned with salt and pepper. Brown on all sides in the oil in a large kettle. Push aside and add the green onions and garlic. Sauté until tender. Add the wine, parsley, bay leaf and thyme. Season with salt and pepper. Bring to a boil. Lower the heat and cook slowly, covered, about 1½ hours, or until the meat is tender. Add the mushrooms and onions 10 minutes before the cooking is finished. Remove and discard the parsley and bay leaf. Serves 6.

Blanquette de Veau

This rich and flavorful well-known dish is made with an inviting combination of veal, small white onions and mushrooms—all served in a lemon-flavored cream sauce.

2½ pounds veal shoulder cut
    into 2-inch cubes
4 cups meat broth or water
1 medium carrot, chopped
1 medium onion stuck with
    2 whole cloves
1 leek, sliced (optional)
1 bouquet garni (bay leaf,
    parsley, thyme)
Salt, pepper to taste

5 tablespoons butter or
    margarine
15 small white onions, peeled
½ cup water
18 medium, fresh mushrooms
2 tablespoons lemon juice
3 tablespoons flour
2 egg yolks
½ cup heavy cream
Freshly grated nutmeg to taste

Put the veal and broth in a large kettle. Bring to a boil and skim. Add the carrot, onion with cloves, leek, *bouquet garni*, salt and pepper. Lower the heat and cook slowly, covered, for 1½ hours, skimming from time to time.

While the veal is cooking, melt 1 tablespoon of butter in a saucepan. Add the white onions and sauté 1 minute. Pour in the water and cook the onions, covered, until just tender, about 10 minutes. Drain and set aside. Clean the mushrooms and cut into halves lengthwise. Sauté in 2 tablespoons of butter and 1 tablespoon of lemon juice for 5 minutes. Remove from the heat and set aside.

When the veal has finished cooking, remove from the stove. Take out the meat. Strain 2 cups of the liquid and set aside. (Discard any remaining liquid and the vegetables). Melt 2 tablespoons of butter in a large saucepan. Add the flour and cook, stirring, 1 minute. Gradually add the strained meat liquid and cook, stirring, until the sauce is thickened and smooth. Combine the egg yolks and cream and beat lightly. Spoon some of the hot sauce to mix with them. Return to the sauce. Cook slowly, stirring often, until thickened. Season with salt, pepper and nutmeg. Add the reserved veal, onions, mushrooms and drippings and the remaining 1 tablespoon of lemon juice. Leave on the stove long enough to heat through. Serves 6.

NOTE: The onions may be arranged as a garnish on top of the stew, if desired.

Alpine Calf's Liver with Mushrooms

An appealing way of serving calf's liver is adapted from a favorite Swiss recipe.

2 pounds calf's liver	2 teaspoons fresh lemon juice
Flour	1 teaspoon drained capers
Salt, pepper to taste	1 cup sour cream, at room
½ cup (about) butter or	temperature
margarine	2 tablespoons chopped fresh
1 medium onion, thinly sliced	parsley
½ pound fresh mushrooms,	
cleaned & sliced	

Cut the liver in ¼ inch slices and then into 2 inch strips. Dust with flour, seasoned with salt and pepper. Heat ⅓ cup of butter in a skillet. Add the liver and quickly fry on both sides until just tender. Remove to a plate and keep warm. Add the onions and more butter to the drippings in the skillet. Sauté until tender. Add the mushrooms and lemon juice and sauté 4 minutes. Mix in the capers and sour cream. Season with salt and pepper. Leave on low heat, stirring, until warmed through. Spoon over the calf's liver. Garnish with the parsley. Serves 4.

Mushroom-Pork Chow Mein

A good buffet dish.

⅓ cup peanut oil
2 medium onions, sliced
½ pound fresh mushrooms,
    cleaned & sliced
1 cup sliced celery
2 cups shredded green
    cabbage
1 can (1 pound) bean
    sprouts, undrained

½ cup sliced bamboo shoots
1 cup cooked pork, cut into
    strips
2 tablespoons cornstarch
⅓ cup soy sauce
¼ cup water
Pepper
Canned chow mein noodles,
    heated

Heat the oil in a large skillet. Add the onions, mushrooms, celery and cabbage and sauté for 5 minutes. Stir in the bean sprouts, bamboo shoots and pork. Mix well. Combine the cornstarch, soy sauce and water and add to the vegetable-pork mixture. Season with pepper. Cook, stirring, until slightly thickened, a few minutes. Do not cook too long as the vegetables should be crisp. Serve over warm chow mein noodles. Serves 6.

Swiss Steak with Mushrooms

This old favorite is made even better by the addition of mushrooms.

2 pounds round steak, about
    1½ inches thick
½ cup flour
Salt, pepper to taste
Fat for frying

1 large onion, sliced thinly
3 cups canned tomatoes
½ pound fresh mushrooms
    cleaned & sliced thickly
¼ cup butter or margarine

Remove any excess fat from the steak and cut into 4 pieces. Dredge with the flour, seasoned with salt and pepper. Pound with a meat hammer or the edge of a heavy plate until about ½ inch thick. Set aside. Use enough fat to lightly grease a large skillet. Add the onion and sauté until tender. Spoon onto a plate. Grease the skillet again. Add the meat and brown on all sides. Spoon the onions over the meat. Add the tomatoes. Cook slowly, covered, 1½ to 2 hours, until the meat is tender. While cooking, sauté the mushrooms in the butter for 4 minutes. Add to the meat 5 minutes before it is finished cooking. Serves 4.

Mushroom Burgers, Texas Style

Serve for an outdoor meal.

2 *pounds lean ground beef*	2 *teaspoons steak sauce*
2 *garlic cloves, crushed*	¼ *cup ketchup*
1 *medium onion, chopped*	*Salt, pepper to taste*
1½ *cups chopped*	16 *medium, fresh mushroom*
mushrooms, fresh or	*caps*
canned	
2 *teaspoons chili powder*	

Combine all the ingredients except the mushroom caps and mix well. Shape into 8 large hamburger patties. Broil or fry to the desired degree of doneness, turning one or two times. Garnish each hamburger with two raw mushroom caps on a tooth pick. Serves 8.

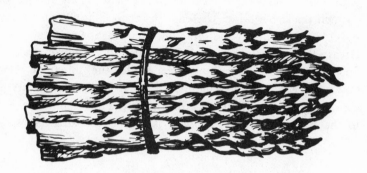

Lamb Mushroom Shish Kebabs

An attractive and appealing dish for an outdoor party.

1½ pounds lean boneless
    lamb, cubed
2 jars (4½ ounces each)
    whole mushrooms,
    drained
⅓ cup olive oil

2 tablespoons lemon juice
¼ teaspoon dried oregano
Salt, pepper to taste
Medium-size green pepper
    pieces

Combine all the ingredients, except the green pepper pieces, in a large bowl. Leave to marinate for 1 to 2 hours, turning now and then. Thread the lamb, mushrooms and green pepper pieces alternately on small skewers. Brush with the marinade. Cook on an outdoor grill or broil, several inches from the heat, turning once or twice, for about 10 minutes. Serves 4 to 6.

Provençale Beef Daube

Another excellent stew from Provence, the lovely southern province of France.

3 pounds stewing beef, cubed
1 cup dry white or red wine
6 tablespoons olive oil
2 large onions, sliced
3 large carrots, diced
2 bay leaves
1 teaspoon dried thyme
1/3 cup chopped parsley
Salt, pepper to taste

1/2 cup diced thick bacon
2 garlic cloves, crushed
3 medium tomatoes, peeled
   & chopped
1 strip orange peel
1/2 teaspoon dried rosemary
1/2 pound fresh mushrooms,
   sliced thickly
12 pitted black olives

Put the beef, wine, 4 tablespoons of oil, 1 onion, 2 carrots, bay leaves, thyme and 2 tablespoons of parsley in a large bowl. Season with salt and pepper. Leave to marinate for about 2 hours. Stir now and then.

When ready to cook, put the bacon, garlic, remaining 2 tablespoons of oil, onion and carrot in a kettle and sauté for 5 minutes. Remove the meat from the marinade, reserving the marinade, and brown, a few pieces at a time. Mix in the tomatoes, orange peel and rosemary. Season with salt and pepper and pour in the marinade, including the vegetables. Cook slowly, covered, for 1 hour. Add the mushrooms and olives during the last 15 minutes of cooking. Mix in the remaining parsley. Serves 6 to 8.

Sauté de Veau Marengo

2½ pounds boneless veal, cut
    into 2 inch cubes
¼ cup flour
Salt, pepper to taste
¼ cup olive oil
1 medium onion, chopped
1 garlic clove, crushed

4 medium tomatoes, peeled
    & chopped
½ teaspoon dried marjoram
Dry white wine
1 pound small fresh
    mushrooms, cleaned
¼ cup butter
¼ cup chopped fresh parsley

Dust the veal cubes with the flour seasoned with salt and pepper. Brown in the oil in a large saucepan or kettle. Push aside and add the onion and garlic. Sauté until tender. Add the tomatoes, marjoram and wine to cover. Cook slowly, covered, about 1 hour, or until the veal is tender. Add more wine while cooking, if needed. Sauté the mushrooms in the butter for 5 minutes. Add, with the parsley, to the veal mixture 5 minutes before the cooking is finished. Serves 6.

Mushroom Meat Loaf

The great family favorite, meat loaf, can be elegantly served for a company meal when enriched by the addition of mushrooms.

½ pound fresh mushrooms,
    chopped
2 tablespoons butter or
    margarine

2 eggs, beaten
½ cup fine dry bread crumbs
½ cup minced onion
½ cup tomato juice

1   tablespoon lemon juice
2   pounds lean ground beef
    (or mixture of beef, pork
    and veal)

½   teaspoon each of dried
    basil and oregano
Salt, pepper to taste
Basic Brown Mushroom Sauce

Sauté the mushrooms in the butter and lemon juice for 4 minutes. Mix with the meat, eggs, bread crumbs, onion, tomato juice, basil, oregano, salt and pepper. Shape into a loaf in a greased shallow dish or loaf pan. Bake in a preheated moderate oven (350°F.) about 1 hour, until done. Serve with Basic Brown Mushroom Sauce (page 205). Serves 6 to 8.

NOTE: A decorative meat loaf can be made by putting whole fresh mushrooms in the center of it. To make, put half the meat mixture in a loaf pan. Make slight indentations lengthwise along the center of the meat. Arrange 6 cleaned whole mushrooms, standing upright, along the center. Cover with the remaining meat.

London Broil with Mushroom Sauce

An excellent steak recipe for a small dinner.

1   flank steak, about 1½
    pounds
⅓   cup peanut oil
3   tablespoons soy sauce
¼   cup dry red wine
2   tablespoons minced shallots
    or green onions
1   garlic clove, crushed
Pepper to taste

3   tablespoons butter
½   pound whole fresh
    mushrooms, cleaned &
    thickly sliced
3   tablespoons butter
3   tablespoons flour
1½ cups beef bouillon
Salt
Freshly grated nutmeg

Cut any fat from the steak. Place the steak in a shallow

dish. Cover with the oil, soy sauce, wine, shallots, garlic and pepper. Leave to marinate for 3 hours, turning occasionally. Broil under high heat allowing about 5 minutes for each side. Remove to a serving dish and keep warm. Spoon any steak drippings into a small skillet. Add the butter and mushrooms and sauté for 4 minutes. Mix in the flour. Gradually add the bouillon and cook slowly, stirring, until the gravy thickens. Season with salt, pepper and nutmeg. To serve, slice the steak very thin, diagonally across the grain. Spoon the sauce over the steak slices. Serves 4.

Korean Chop Chay

In Korea a favorite dish is named *chop chay*, which means a combination of chopped ingredients which are cooked very quickly and well seasoned with the traditional soy sauce and sesame seeds.

2 pounds boneless round steak
   or sirloin
2 garlic cloves, crushed
12 green onions, including
   tops, cut into 1-inch
   lengths
½ cup soy sauce
2 tablespoons toasted sesame
   seeds*
Pepper to taste
½ cup (about) peanut oil
3 medium carrots, finely
   chopped

2 medium onions, finely
   chopped
2 cups chopped spinach
   leaves, washed and
   trimmed
1 pound fresh mushrooms,
   cleaned & sliced
2 cans (1 pound each) bean
   sprouts, drained
4 bamboo shoots, sliced
½ pound fine egg noodles or
   vermicelli

Cut the meat into thin strips about 3 inches long. Put in a large bowl with the garlic, green onions, soy sauce and sesame seeds. Season with pepper. Mix well and leave to marinate for 1 hour, stirring occasionally.

When ready to cook, heat 3 tablespoons of the oil in a large skillet. Add the meat and marinade and cook a few minutes, until the meat is tender. Remove to a plate and keep warm. Add more oil, the carrots and onions and sauté for 5 minutes. Remove to a plate and keep warm. Add the spinach, mushrooms, bean sprouts, bamboo shoots and more oil to the skillet and sauté for 4 minutes. Return the meat, carrots and onions and any juices to the skillet. Leave over very low heat. Cook the noodles and drain. Stir into the meat-vegetable mixture. Mix well and leave on the heat just long enough to warm through. Serves 8.

*To toast sesame seeds, sauté in a pan over low heat until nut brown.

New England Creamed Dried Beef with Mushrooms

½ pound dried beef,
    shredded
¼ cup butter
1 small onion, minced
1 can (6 to 8 ounces)
    mushroom stems and
    pieces, drained

1 can (10½ ounces)
    condensed cream of
    mushroom soup
1½ cups milk
Freshly grated nutmeg, pepper
    to taste
Toast points
3 tablespoons chopped fresh
    parsley

Fry the beef in the butter in a large saucepan for 5 minutes. Add the onion and sauté until tender. Stir in the mushrooms and sauté for 4 minutes. Add the soup, milk, nutmeg and pepper and cook slowly, stirring, until warmed through. Serve over toast points garnished with the parsley. Serves 4.

German Knockwurst and Sauerkraut with Mushrooms

A good winter supper dish.

1 medium onion, chopped
3 tablespoons fat
2 cans (1 pound each) sauerkraut, drained
2 tart apples, peeled, cored and chopped
2 cans (8 ounces each) tomato sauce with mushrooms

½ teaspoon dried thyme
1 bay leaf
Salt, pepper to taste
1 can (6 to 8 ounces) sliced mushrooms, drained
8 knockwurst

Sauté the onion in the fat in a large saucepan until tender. Add the sauerkraut and sauté, mixing with a fork, for 1 minute. Add the apples, sauce, thyme, bay leaf, salt and pepper. Bring to a boil. Lower the heat and cook slowly, covered, for 20 minutes. Add the drained mushrooms and knockwurst and cook 10 minutes longer. Remove and discard the bay leaf. Serves 6 to 8.

Creamed Sweetbreads with Mushrooms

1 pair large sweetbreads
Juice of 1 medium lemon
6 tablespoons butter or margarine

½ pound fresh mushrooms, cleaned & sliced
3 tablespoons flour
2 cups light cream or milk

1 cup sliced green onions,
    with tops

⅓ cup dry sherry
Grated fresh nutmeg to taste
Salt, pepper to taste

Precook the sweetbreads by simmering in salted water to cover, with juice of 1 lemon added, for 20 minutes. Remove the outer membranes, veins and connective tissues. Break into pieces. Melt the butter in a skillet or saucepan. Add the onions and sauté until tender. Add the mushrooms and sauté 4 minutes. Stir in the flour. Gradually add the cream and cook slowly, stirring, until thickened. Add the sweetbreads, sherry, nutmeg, salt and pepper. Leave on the heat just long enough to warm through. Serve on toast points if desired. Serves 4.

Mushroom-Stuffed Flank Steaks

An attractive creation for a company meal.

2 flank steaks, about 1½
    pounds each
Meat tenderizer
¼ cup vinegar
¼ cup soy sauce
¼ cup dry sherry
Pepper to taste

1½ cups minced green
    onions, with tops
3 tablespoons butter or
    margarine
1¼ cups chopped fresh
    mushrooms
¼ cup chopped parsley
Salt to taste

Cut the narow ends from the steaks so they will be even. Prick the meat with a fork and sprinkle with the tenderizer. Place in a shallow dish and cover with the vinegar, soy sauce and sherry. Sprinkle with pepper. Leave to marinate for about 2 hours, turning occasionally. Sauté the onions in the butter until tender. Add the mushrooms and sauté for 4 minutes. Mix in the parsley. Season with salt and pepper. Remove the steaks to a flat surface, reserving the marinade. Spoon the mushroom mixture along the center of each steak. Roll up, and holding tightly, cut, slightly diagonally, with a sharp knife into 1½ to 2 inch slices. Carefully string on skewers and brush with the marinade. Broil, turning once, about 10 minutes, or until desired degree of doneness. While preparing, be careful that the stuffing does not fall out. Serve on the skewers. Serves 6 to 8.

Japanese Sukiyaki

This Japanese dish which has become so popular in the United States is made traditionally in a flat-bottomed iron pot, but a thick skillet can be used as a substitute.

1¼ cups soy sauce
1¼ cups sake or dry white wine
⅓ cup sugar
1½ teaspoons monosodium glutamate
1 cup (about) vegetable oil
3 pounds beef sirloin, thinly sliced

3 medium onions, thinly sliced
8 green onions, cut into 3-inch lengths
½ pound fresh mushrooms, sliced
1 cup sliced bamboo shoots

Combine the soy sauce, *sake*, sugar and monosodium glutamate. Pour into a pitcher and set aside. Add enough oil to grease a sukiyaki cooker or skillet. With chopsticks or a fork, dip the meat slices, a few at a time, into the soy-*sake* mixture and spread over the surface of the skillet. Brown and push aside. Add the vegetables and a generous portion of the soy-*sake* mixture. Cook, turning, until just tender. Do not overcook as the vegetables should be crisp. Serves 8.

Polish Hunters' Stew

This favorite Polish stew, called *Bigos* and made with a wide variety of meats and poultry, was traditional fare for a party following a hunt. Because of the number of ingredients it was generally made in large quantities and took days to prepare. This is a simple version which could be served for a buffet meal.

3 ounces dried mushrooms
¼ pound salt pork or bacon, diced
2 large onions, sliced
3 pounds mixed roasted or boiled meats (pork, veal, game or poultry), cubed

3 pounds sauerkraut, drained
½ pound Polish sausage, sliced
½ cup Madeira wine
Sugar, salt, pepper to taste
Vegetable broth or water

Soak the mushrooms in lukewarm water to cover for 20 minutes. Drain the mushrooms, pressing them to release all the liquids. Reserve the liquid and slice the mushrooms. Cook the salt pork in a large kettle and fry the onions in it. Add the mushrooms, meats, sauerkraut, sausage, Madeira, sugar, salt and pepper. Pour in the reserved mushroom liquid and enough broth or water to cover. Bring to a boil. Lower the heat and cook slowly, covered, for 1 hur. Serves 8 to 10.

Boeuf à la Bourguignonne

This savory *ragoût*, listed on menus generally as *boeuf bourguignon*, is one of the most famous of the French dishes. For a company meal it may be prepared beforehand and reheated.

3 *pounds boneless stewing beef cut into 2-inch cubes*
4 *thick slices of bacon, chopped*
1 *tablespoon of olive oil*
1 *medium carrot, sliced*
1 *medium onion, sliced*
1 *leek, sliced (optional)*
2 *tablespoons flour*
2 *garlic cloves, crushed*
1 *bouquet garni (bay leaf, parsley, thyme)*
2½ *cups dry red wine*
2½ *cups beef stock or bouillon*
Salt, pepper to taste
24 *small white onions*
4 *tablespoons butter*
⅔ *cup water*
1 *pound fresh mushrooms*
1 *tablespoon tomato paste*

Wipe the beef dry. Heat the bacon and oil in a large kettle. Add the beef, a few cubes at a time, and brown on all sides. Remove with a slotted spoon to a plate. Add the carrot, onion and leek to the drippings and sauté 2 minutes. Return the beef to the kettle. Sprinkle with the flour. Mix well. Add the garlic, *bouquet garni*, wine and stock. Season with salt and pepper and bring to a boil. Lower the heat and cook slowly, covered, about 1½ hours, or until the meat is tender.

While the meat is cooking, sauté the onions in 1 tablespoon of butter in a saucepan for 1 minute. Add the water and cook, covered, until just tender, about 10 minutes. Clean the mushrooms and cut in half lengthwise. Sauté in 3 tablespoons of butter for 5 minutes. Ten minutes before the meat is finished cooking, stir in the tomato paste. Add the onions and mushrooms, with the drippings, just before removing from the heat. Serves 6.

Mushroom-Stuffed Pork Chops with Yogurt Sauce

An interesting entrée for a company meal.

1 medium onion, chopped
5 tablespoons butter or
   margarine
2 teaspoons lemon juice
½ pound fresh mushrooms,
   cleaned and chopped
½ cup small stale white
   bread cubes

2 tablespoons chopped parsley
   or dill
Salt, pepper to taste
6 thick center-cut loin pork
   chops
½ teaspoon dried rosemary
2 tablespoons flour
2 cup plain yogurt

Sauté the onion in 3 tablespoons of butter in a saucepan until tender. Add the lemon juice and mushrooms, and sauté 4 minutes. Mix in the bread cubes and parsley. Season with salt and pepper. Remove from the heat. Cut any excess fat from the chops, reserving 2 or 3 pieces of the fat. With a sharp knife make a slit lengthwise as deep as possible in each chop to make a pocket. Sprinkle inside and out with salt and pepper. Carefully spoon the stuffing into the pockets. Close with toothpicks or small skewers. Fry the reserved pieces of fat in a large skillet to grease it lightly. Brown each chop on both sides in the skillet, turning carefully so the stuffing does not come out. Arrange all the chops in the skillet. Sprinkle with rosemary, salt and pepper. Add a little water. Braise, covered, over low heat about 1 hour, or until the chops are well cooked. Check now and then to see if more water is needed. When cooked, remove the chops from the skillet and keep warm in the oven. Scrape the drippings.

Stir in the remaining 2 tablespoons of butter and then the flour. Gradually add the yogurt and cook over low heat, stirring, about 5 minutes, until the sauce is thickened. Serve with the chops. Serves 6.

Creamed Ham and Mushrooms on Corn Muffins

This easy-to-prepare dish is good for a brunch or luncheon.

3 tablespoons butter
1 cup sliced mushrooms,
    fresh or canned
3 tablespoons flour
2 cups light cream or milk

2 teaspoons prepared mustard
Salt, pepper to taste
2 cups diced cooked ham
6 warm corn muffins, cut into
    halves

Melt the butter in a saucepan. Add the mushrooms and sauté for 4 minutes. Stir in the flour. Add the cream and cook slowly, stirring, until the mixture thickens. Add the mustard, salt, pepper and ham. Cook 5 minutes. Serve over the muffins. Serves 6.

Veal Marsala with Mushrooms

½ pound fresh mushrooms,
    cleaned & sliced
6 tablespoons butter
1½ pounds thin veal escallops
Juice of 1 medium lemon

Flour
Salt, pepper to taste
3 tablespoons olive or salad oil
Marsala wine
⅓ cup chopped fresh parsley

Sauté the mushrooms in 3 tablespoons of butter for 4 minutes. Remove from the heat and keep warm. Sprinkle the veal escallops with the lemon juice. Dust with flour. Season with salt and pepper. Heat the remaining 3 tablespoons of butter and the oil in a skillet. Add the escallops and sauté 2 or 3 minutes on each side, until tender. Add the sautéed mushrooms and cover with wine. Leave on the stove long enough to heat through. Remove the escallops and keep warm. Add ⅓ cup wine to the skillet and bring to a boil. Pour over the meat. Serve garnished with the parsley. Serves 4.

Salads and Vegetables

Over the centuries culinary fashions have been as varied as any others which pertain to our daily living customs. The vogue for particular salads and vegetables has fluctuated so remarkably that some of our contemporary favorites would once have been considered suspect or unacceptable. Mushrooms, served both as salads and vegetables, have figured prominently on the gastronomic roster and have been held suspect at one time, deemed wonderful at another. Fortunately, they have triumphed in the latter role.

The primary reasons both for skepticism and wonderment about mushrooms were a lack of knowledge about their growth and about their botanical relatives. Ancient man dined on whatever edible plants he could forage. The roots, seeds, bulbs, stems, pods, leaves and flowers were boiled by themselves or cooked with other foods. With the cultivation of wild plants came an increase in the variety and amount available for food. In ancient Asia Minor, the earliest salads were made of greens and vegetables dressed with olive or sesame oil, vinegar, lemon juice, herbs or spices. As man's gastronomic knowledge increased, he became curious about the origins of foods and attempted to classify them into various categories. Mushrooms were, from the first, a great botanical mystery since they did not grow like other plants. Also, it was soon discovered that some were edible and others were poisonous.

Mushrooms fascinated an early Greek food writer by the name of Theophrastus, who warned his readers about the dangers of eating the wrong kinds. About their appearance he wrote that they ". . . grow without any roots; but the real mushrooms have, as the beginning by which they adhere to the ground, a stalk of some length, and they put forth fibres from that stalk . . ." He also noted that some kinds appeared on the sea shore "close to high-water mark, which they say are left there by the sun."

Despite the mystery, the early Greeks enjoyed them roasted or served dressed with "vinegar or honey and vinegar, or honey, or salt." In the earliest classical discourses on cookery, mushroom recipes were listed under "gourmet foods" or along with vegetables. The French served them as accompaniments to their favorite meat and poultry dishes. In Elizabethan England, mushrooms were sometimes mixed with greens and herbs to make "sallets."

In early America, where our forefathers were learning about New World plants and attempting to cultivate some Old World favorites, there were skeptics who scorned native foods such as tomatoes and mushrooms. About the latter, an eighteenth century cookbook author wrote, "Have nothing to do with them until you are an excellent judge between the true and false . . . Not being ambitious of martyrdom, even in the cause of gastronomical enterprise, especially if the instrument is to be a contemptible, rank-smelling fungus, I never eat or cook mushrooms."

Today, with our great abundance of cultivated mushrooms, there is no fear of eating them, and their gastronomic merits are widely extolled. Mushrooms are not actually vegetables, although many recipes for them are still included in that category. But on the other hand, neither are such fruits as cucumbers, squash or tomatoes, which are also served as vegetables.

Nomenclature aside, mushrooms are gastronomic treats when served by themselves or with other vegetables and seasonings as salads or accompaniments. To each of these dishes they lend a subtle refinement proving that the magic of their goodness has long ago erased any unpleasant associations from the past.

German Vegetable Salad

Serve with pork, poultry or game.

1 package (10 ounces)
   frozen cauliflower
1½ cups cooked peas
½ pound fresh mushrooms,
   cleaned & sliced
½ cup sour cream

1 tablespoon lemon juice
¼ teaspoon paprika
1 tablespoon chopped fresh
   dill or parsley
Salt, pepper to taste

Cook the cauliflower and drain. Cut into bite-size pieces.
Mix with the peas and mushrooms. Combine the remaining ingredients and mix with the vegetables. Chill. Serves 6.

Belgian Endive with Mushroom Dressing

Imported endive is a delicacy to serve for a special company
meal. This mushroom dressing enhances its appearance and
flavor.

3 heads Belgian endive
½ cup mayonnaise
⅓ cup sour cream
¼ cup ketchup

1½ cups chopped fresh
   mushrooms
1 tablespoon fresh lemon
   juice
Salt, pepper, cayenne to taste

Wash the endive and wipe dry. Cut each head lengthwise
into halves. Combine the remaining ingredients and spoon over
the endive. Chill. Serves 6.

Orange Mushroom Salad

A good salad for a ladies' luncheon.

½ cup seedless raisins
3 seedless oranges
½ pound fresh mushrooms,
  cleaned & sliced thickly

1 cup coarsely shredded raw
  carrots
3 cups mixed salad greens
½-¾ cup French dressing

Boil the raisins in water to cover for 5 minutes. Drain and cool. Peel the oranges and separate into sections. Mix the raisins and oranges with the remaining ingredients, adding as much dressing as desired. Mix well. Serves 6.

West Coast Salad Bowl

Serve with meat or poultry for an outdoor meal.

1 small head Iceberg lettuce
1 bunch escarole
1 jar (4½ ounces) sliced
  mushrooms, drained
1 medium-size, ripe avocado

¼ cup fresh lemon juice
½ cup salad oil
1 teaspoon sugar
½ teaspoon dry mustard
Salt, pepper to taste

Wash the lettuce and escarole. Dry. Remove the core of the lettuce and the roots of the escarole. Break into bite-size pieces. Put in a large salad bowl. Add the mushrooms. Peel the avocado and take out the stone. Cut the pulp into small pieces. Sprinkle with lemon juice and mix with the remaining ingredients. Add to the lettuce mixture and toss lightly. Serves 6 to 8.

Low Calorie Mushroom Salad

A delicious salad which might appeal to weight-watchers.

1 pound fresh mushrooms,
    cleaned & sliced
1 cup diced celery
1 cup diced green pepper
2 tablespoons sliced green
    onions

¼ cup olive oil
3 tablespoons fresh lemon
    juice or vinegar
Salt, pepper to taste

Combine the ingredients and mix well. Chill. Serves 6.

Italian Artichoke-Mushroom Salad

Serve with pasta, veal or pork.

1 package (9 ounces) frozen
    artichoke hearts
2 cups sliced fresh
    mushrooms
1 large tomato, peeled &
    diced

1 garlic clove, crushed
½ teaspoon dried basil
¼ teaspoon dried oregano
3 tablespoons olive oil
2 tablespoons lemon juice
Salt, pepper to taste

Cook the artichoke hearts and drain. Cut into halves length-wise and cool. Mix in a bowl with the mushrooms and tomato. Combine the remaining ingredients and pour over the vegetables. Serves 4.

Mushroom-Watercress Salad

The pungent flavor of watercress combines well with the mildness of mushrooms to make a simple but inviting salad.

2 cups washed and drained
    watercress
2 cups sliced raw mushrooms

½ cup sliced green onions
½ cup French dressing

Arrange the watercress in the center of a plate. Put the slices of mushrooms and green onions over it. Pour the dressing over the vegetables. Serves 6.

Spinach Mushroom Salad

Serve with seafood or beef.

10 ounces fresh spinach
½ pound fresh mushrooms,
    cleaned & sliced
½ cup sliced green onions
6 tablespoons olive or salad
    oil

Juice of 1 small lemon
1 garlic clove, crushed
⅛ teaspoon dry mustard
Salt, pepper to taste
6 strips thin bacon, fried crisp
    and crumbled

Trim and wash the spinach. Discard any stems. Dry well and put in a salad bowl. Add the mushrooms and onions and toss. Combine the oil, lemon juice, garlic, mustard, salt and pepper and pour over the salad. Toss. Sprinkle the bacon over the top. Serves 6.

Baked Green Beans and Mushrooms

An easy-to-prepare accompaniment for hamburgers or frank-furters.

½ pound fresh mushrooms, cleaned & sliced
3 tablespoons butter or margarine
2 packages (9 ounces each) frozen cut green beans, cooked & drained

1 can (10½ ounces) condensed cream of mushroom soup
½ cup milk
Salt, pepper to taste
Grated Parmesan cheese

Sauté the mushrooms in the butter for 4 minutes. Combine with the remaining ingredients, except the cheese, and turn into a buttered shallow baking dish. Sprinkle the top with cheese. Bake in a preheated moderate oven (350°F.) for 20 minutes. Serves 6.

German Potatoes and Mushrooms

A good accompaniment for pork.

4 medium potatoes
4 slices bacon, cut into 1-inch pieces
1 medium onion, chopped
2 cups sliced raw mushrooms

½ cup sour cream at room temperature
Salt, pepper to taste
2 tablespoons chopped parsley

Peel the potatoes and boil in salted water until just tender.

Cool and cut into thin slices. Fry the bacon until crisp. Spoon off all except 3 tablespoons of the fat. Add the onion and sauté until tender. Add the mushrooms and sauté 4 minutes. Stir in the sour cream. Add the potatoes, salt and pepper and leave on the heat long enough to warm through. Garnish with parsley. Serves 4.

Bohemian Mushroom Goulash

A good accompaniment for pork, poultry, or beef.

1/4 cup butter or margarine
1 medium onion, chopped
1 tablespoon paprika
1 pound fresh mushrooms,
    cleaned & sliced

3 large tomatoes, peeled &
    chopped
1 large green pepper, cleaned
    & chopped
Salt, pepper to taste
2 teaspoons chopped fresh dill

Melt the butter in a skillet, and sauté the onion in it until tender. Add the paprika and cook 1 minute. Stir in the mushrooms, 1/2 pound at a time, and sauté for 4 minutes. Add the tomatoes, green pepper, salt and pepper, and cook gently for 5 minutes. Stir in the dill and remove from the heat. Serves 4 to 6.

Deep-Fried Mushrooms

Serve as an accompaniment to meat or poultry.

1 pound medium-size, fresh
    mushrooms
1/4 cup flour
Salt, white pepper to taste

2 eggs, beaten
3/4 cup fine dry bread crumbs
Fat for frying

Clean the mushrooms and wipe dry. Combine the flour, salt and pepper and dredge the mushrooms in it. Dip them in beaten egg. Roll in bread crumbs. Fry in hot deep fat (365°F. on a frying thermometer) about 3 minutes. Drain on paper toweling. Serves 6.

Central European Baked Sauerkraut and Dried Mushrooms

Serve as an accompaniment to pork or game.

1 ounce dried mushrooms	1 large tart apple, peeled &
4 slices bacon, chopped	chopped
1 medium onion, chopped	½ teaspoon dried thyme
1 quart bulk sauerkraut,	Salt, pepper to taste
drained	1 can or bottle (12 ounces)
	beer

Soak the mushrooms in lukewarm water to cover for 20 minutes. Drain, pressing to extract all the liquid. Chop. Fry the bacon and onion until the bacon is crisp and the onion is tender. Mix with the mushrooms, sauerkraut, apple, thyme, salt and pepper and spoon into a shallow baking dish. Pour the beer over the ingredients. Bake, covered, in a preheated moderate oven (350°F.) for 50 minutes. Serves 4 to 6.

Marinated Mushrooms and Artichokes from Corsica

Some of the world's best artichokes are grown on the lovely Mediterranean island of Corsica where they are mixed with mushrooms and served as an accompaniment to meats and poultry.

1 *package (9 ounces) frozen artichoke hearts*	3 *tablespoons olive oil*
1/2 *pound fresh mushrooms, cleaned*	1/4 *teaspoon dried oregano*
Juice of 1 medium lemon	1/4 *teaspoon dried basil*
	1 *garlic clove, crushed*
	Salt, pepper to taste

Cook the artichoke hearts until just tender. Cut into halves lengthwise. Drain and cool. Slice the mushrooms through the stems into halves. Combine with the artichokes. Add the remaining ingredients. Leave to marinate for 2 hours. Serves 4.

Italian Stuffed Mushrooms

An excellent accompaniment for meats or poultry.

1 *pound medium-size, fresh mushrooms*	1/2 *cup minced prosciutto or ham*
1/4 *cup fresh lemon juice*	2 *tablespoons grated Parmesan cheese*
1 *cup soft bread crumbs*	1/2 *teaspoon dried oregano*
3/4 *cup canned Italian plum tomatoes, drained & chopped*	1 *tablespoon parsley flakes*
	1 *garlic clove, crushed*
	1/4 *cup olive or salad oil*

Clean the mushrooms and gently pull off the stems. Use the stems for another dish. Dip each cap in lemon juice. Combine the remaining ingredients, except the oil, and mix well. Fill each cap with a spoonful of the tomato-bread crumb mixture. Arrange the stuffed caps in a buttered shallow baking dish. Sprinkle the oil over them. Pour a little hot water into the dish. Bake in a preheated hot oven (400°F.) for 15 minutes. Serves 6.

Oriental Peas and Mushrooms

½ pound fresh mushrooms
1 can (5 ounces) bamboo
    shoots
1 tablespoon peanut or salad
    oil
1 package (10 ounces) frozen
    green peas

2 teaspoons soy sauce
1 vegetable bouillon cube
½ cup hot water
3 tablespoons cornstarch
⅓ cup cold water
Slivered almonds

Clean the mushrooms and slice from the round sides through the stems. Drain and slice the bamboo shoots. Melt the oil in a skillet. Add the peas and break apart with a fork. Add the soy sauce, bouillon cube, hot water, mushrooms and bamboo shoots. Cook, stirring often, for 5 minutes. Mix the cornstarch with the cold water and stir into the vegetables. Cook, stirring, until the liquid is thickened and the ingredients are cooked. Serve sprinkled with the slivered almonds. Serves 4.

Caraway Mushrooms in Sour Cream

Serve with pork, poultry or game.

1 pound fresh mushrooms or
    2 cans (6 or 8 ounces
    each) sliced mushrooms
¼ cup butter or margarine
½ cup minced onion
2 teaspoons caraway seed

2 teaspoons lemon juice
¼ cup flour
Salt, pepper to taste
½ cup milk
1 cup sour cream at room
    temperature

Clean and slice the fresh mushrooms, or drain them if canned. Heat the butter in a large skillet. Add the onion and sauté until tender. Add the mushrooms, caraway seed and lemon juice and sauté for 4 minutes. Mix in the flour, salt and pepper. Pour in the milk. Stir well and cook 1 minute. Add the sour cream and leave on the stove just long enough to heat through. Serves 6.

Mushrooms Baked in Foil

A good dish to serve at an outdoor meal.

Line a shallow baking dish with aluminum foil. Place 1 pound cleaned fresh mushrooms, caps down, on the foil. Sprinkle with lemon juice, chopped parsley, salt and pepper. Cover with another sheet of foil and seal tightly. Bake in a preheated moderate oven (350°F.) for 20 minutes. Serves 4.

Mediterranean Eggplant-Mushroom Medley

A flavorful accompaniment for lamb, chicken or fish.

1 medium eggplant	2 medium onions, sliced
¾ to 1 cup olive oil	1-2 garlic cloves, crushed
1 can (1 pound) plum tomatoes	1 tablespoon chopped fresh parsley
1 jar (4½ ounces) sliced mushrooms, drained	1 teaspoon drained capers
	Salt, pepper to taste

Remove the stem from the eggplant and cut the eggplant into cubes. Sauté them in oil until soft. Add the other ingredients and cook slowly, uncovered, stirring now and then, until the vegetables are cooked, about 20 minutes. Serves 6.

Spinach and Mushrooms, Japanese Style

Serve with beef or chicken.

½ pound spinach, washed
½ pound fresh mushrooms, cleaned & sliced
¼ cup toasted sesame seeds*
¼ cup soy sauce
Pepper to taste
¼ teaspoon ajinomoto (monosodium glutamate)

Cook the spinach until tender in just the water that clings to the leaves after washing. Drain. Mix with the remaining ingredients and serve cold. Serves 4.

*To toast the sesame seeds, fry in a skillet until they become brown.

Cèpes à la Bordelaise

The flavor of imported cèpes is here enhanced by the addition of a few fine ingredients. Serve with beef or veal.

1 can (10 ounces) cèpes
5 tablespoons oil
1 garlic clove, crushed
1 tablespoon chopped fresh parsley
1 tablespoon chopped shallots
Salt, freshly ground pepper to taste

Wash the cèpes in cold water. Drain and wipe dry. Slice thickly. Heat the oil in a skillet. Add the cèpes and sauté 2 minutes. Drain. Add the other ingredients and mix well. Serves 4.

Rumanian Leeks and Mushrooms

Serve with eggs, meat or poultry.

6 leeks
½ pound fresh mushrooms
Juice of 1 lemon
2 tablespoons butter
2 tablespoons flour

1½ cups milk
2 tablespoons chopped dill
Salt, pepper to taste
Grated Parmesan cheese

Wash the leeks thoroughly to remove all the dirt. Cut off and discard the tops. Slice the white parts into halves lengthwise. Cut into 1 inch pieces. Cook in salted water to cover until tender, about 10 minutes. Use a slotted spoon to remove to a shallow baking dish. Clean the mushrooms and slice. Arrange over the leeks. Sprinkle with the lemon juice. Melt the butter in a saucepan. Stir in the flour. Add the milk and cook slowly, stirring, until smooth and thickened. Add the dill, salt and pepper. Pour over the leeks and mushrooms. Sprinkle the top with grated Parmesan. Put under the broiler until hot and bubbly. Serves 4.

Asparagus and Mushrooms Polonaise

Serve with beef or chicken.

1 pound fresh asparagus
1 can (4 ounces) sliced
    mushrooms, drained
½ cup dry bread crumbs

⅓ cup butter or margarine
1½ tablespoons lemon juice
Salt, pepper to taste

Wash and trim the asparagus. Cook in a little salted water, covered, until tender, about 10 minutes. Drain and arrange in a shallow buttered baking dish. Place the sliced mushrooms over the asparagus. Sauté the bread crumbs in the butter and lemon juice until golden. Season with salt and pepper. Spoon over the asparagus and mushrooms. Put under the broiler until hot and bubbly. Serves 4.

Mushroom Stuffed-Tomatoes

This flavorful creation may be served as an accompaniment to meat, poultry or seafood, as an appetizer, or as a first course.

4 medium tomatoes
¼ cup minced green onions,
    with tops
2 tablespoons butter or
    margarine

½ cup tiny stale bread cubes
1 cup sautéed mushrooms
Salt, pepper, nutmeg to taste

Cut a slice from the top of each tomato. Spoon out and discard the pulp and liquid. Invert each tomato to drain. Sauté the onions in the butter until tender. Add the bread cubes and sauté until golden. Remove from the heat and mix with the sautéed mushrooms, salt, pepper and nutmeg. Spoon into the tomato shells. Set in a shallow baking dish. Add a little hot water. Bake in a preheated moderate oven (350°F.) for about 30 minutes. Serves 4.

Sauces and Stuffings

In the realm of cookery, sauces and stuffings do not generally have much in common. We utilize the former to enhance the flavor of various foods and to make them more attractive. The latter are savory mixtures of compatible ingredients which are used as fillings for poultry, seafood, meats and vegetables. Both sauces and stuffings, however, share an affinity for mushrooms.

The triumph of a dish may often be attributed to the selection and preparation of the sauce. Generally speaking, the word means a seasoned liquid and derives from the Latin *saltus*, or salted. But the repertoire of hundreds of sauces includes those which are simple or complex, hot or cold, sweet or unsweetened, and are of many colors and ingredients. They are used to complement all our foods.

Some culinary experts consider the art of sauce-making the most important element of cookery. It took, however, a long time for this expertise to develop. The first sauces were probably those made with the meat juices dripping from roasts, but early man also combined honey, oil and wine with herbs and other seasonings to add flavor to his fare. The Greeks presumably did not think that making sauces was too difficult; for an early writer proclaimed that boiling sauces was "anybody's task; he who does this is but a seasoner and broth-maker."

The Imperial Romans were very fond of pungent sweet and sour sauces which served more to smother or disguise the flavor of foods than to enhance them. The spicy relishes or condiments which later became great favorites in North European countries had much the same purpose. One of these, mushroom ketchup, is still popular fare in Great Britain and Ireland.

The art of sauce-making was perfected by French chefs, and their hundreds of classic creations are still considered to be the world's best. "One can learn to cook, and one can be taught to roast, but a good sauce-maker is a genius born, not made," declared Brillat-Savarin, the eminent French gastronome. Two of the most inventive French sauces were *sauce aux champignons* and one made with *duxelles*, a sautéed preparation of chopped mushrooms and seasonings (see page 45).

Over the years, housewives and cooks in other lands learned to make sauces which were good although perhaps not as complex as those of the French cuisine. The writer of an American cookbook, "Common Sense in the Household of 1871", declared that sauces "are no longer the appendages of the rich man's bill of fare only." The author encouraged her readers to learn how to make them and specified one sauce using "1 teacupful young mushrooms."

The modern cook is fortunate in that making good sauces, to which mushrooms lend added appeal, has been simplified by the large number of fine, readily available bouillons, consommés, gravies and other convenience foods.

Early American stuffings were generally limited to "breadcrumbs, butter, pepper, salt, etc.", as one cookbook described a filling for roast chicken. Over the years, however, our inventive cooks have created a much wider repertoire of stuffings using grains, vegetables, meats, pasta, nuts and a variety of seasonings. It is now possible to prepare family and company meals choosing from a wide variety of entrées filled with inviting stuffings to which mushrooms make a notable contribution.

Basic White Mushroom Sauce

Serve with eggs, vegetables, poultry, pasta or rice.

½ pound fresh mushrooms,
   cleaned & thinly sliced
5 tablespoons butter or
   margarine
2 teaspoons fresh lemon juice

3 tablespoons flour
2½ cups milk
Freshly grated nutmeg to taste
   (optional)
Salt, white pepper to taste

Sauté the mushrooms in 2 tablespoons of butter and the lemon juice for 4 minutes. Remove from the heat and set aside. Melt the remaining 3 tablespoons of butter in a saucepan. Stir in the flour and cook, stirring, about 1 minute. Gradually add the milk and cook slowly, stirring, until thickened and smooth. Add the sautéed mushrooms and butter drippings, nutmeg, salt and pepper. Makes about 3 cups.

NOTE: For a thicker sauce, use 2 cups of milk.

Basic Brown Mushroom Sauce

Serve with meat or game.

½ pound fresh mushrooms,
   cleaned
2 tablespoons minced onion
6 tablespoons butter or
   margarine

Salt, pepper to taste
2 teaspoons fresh lemon juice
Beef bouillon (about 1¼
   cups)
3 tablespoons flour

Carefully pull the stems from the mushrooms. Mince the

stems and set aside. Slice the mushroom caps thinly and set aside. Sauté the onion in 1 tablespoon of butter in a saucepan until tender. Add the minced stems and sauté for 2 minutes. Pour in 1½ cups of water. Season with salt and pepper. Bring to a boil. Lower the heat and cook over medium heat for 10 minutes. Strain, pressing the mushroom stems to extract all their liquid. Combine the strained mushroom liquid with enough beef bouillon to make 2½ cups. Set aside. Melt 2 tablespoons of butter in a skillet. Add the lemon juice and sliced mushrooms and sauté for 4 minutes. Remove from the heat and set aside. Melt the remaining 3 tablespoons of butter in a saucepan. Stir in the flour and cook, stirring, about 1 minute. Gradually add the 2½ cups of mushroom-bouillon liquid. Cook slowly, stirring, until the sauce is thickened and smooth. Add the sautéed sliced mushrooms, salt and pepper. Leave on the stove long enough to heat through. Makes about 3 cups.

Mushroom Wine Sauce

Serve with meat, poultry or game.

¼ cup chopped shallots or
    green onions
3 tablespoons butter or
    margarine
2 tablespoons flour
2 cups beef bouillon

2 cups chopped mushrooms,
    fresh or canned
1 tablespoon tomato paste
½ cup dry red wine
1 tablespoon chopped fresh
    parsley
Salt, pepper to taste

Sauté the shallots in the butter until tender. Stir in the flour and cook 1 minute. Gradually add the bouillon and cook slowly, stirring, until thickened and smooth. Add the remaining ingredients. Mix well and cook another 10 minutes. Makes about 3 cups.

Swiss Cheese Mushroom Sauce

Serve with vegetables, hard-cooked eggs, pasta or rice.

2 cups chopped fresh
    mushrooms
5 tablespoons butter or
    margarine
2 teaspoons lemon juice

3 tablespoons flour
2½ cups milk
½ cup grated Swiss cheese
½ teaspoon paprika
Salt, pepper to taste

Sauté the mushrooms in 2 tablespoons of butter and the lemon juice for 4 minutes. Remove from the heat and set aside. Melt the remaining 3 tablespoons of butter in a saucepan. Stir in the flour and cook, stirring, 1 minute. Gradually add the milk and cook slowly, stirring, until smooth and thickened. Add the cheese, paprika, salt and pepper and cook over low heat until the cheese is melted. Makes about 3 cups.

Mushroom Cocktail Sauce

Serve with seafood.

¾ cup chili sauce
¾ cup ketchup
1 cup chopped fresh
    mushrooms
2 tablespoons fresh lemon
    juice

2 tablespoons prepared
    horseradish
Few drops Tabasco sauce
Salt, pepper to taste

Combine all the ingredients and mix well. Chill. Makes about 2¾ cups.

Oriental Sweet-Sour Mushroom Sauce

Serve with pork, poultry or game.

4 dried black mushrooms
2 tablespoons butter or
    margarine
½ cup cider vinegar
1 cup water
2-3 tablespoons soy sauce

¼ cup sugar
2 tablespoons cornstarch
1 tablespoon dry sherry
    (optional)
Pepper to taste

Soak the mushrooms in lukewarm water to cover for 20 minutes. Drain, pressing the mushrooms to release all the liquid. Chop finely. Melt the butter in the saucepan. Add the mushrooms and sauté 1 minute. Combine the remaining ingredients and add to the mushrooms. Cook slowly, stirring frequently, until the sauce is thickened, about 10 minutes. Makes about 2 cups.

Italian Mushroom-Tomato Spaghetti Sauce

Serve with spaghetti or any other kind of pasta.

¼ cup olive oil
1 garlic clove, crushed
1 cup chopped onion
1 can (32 ounces) Italian
    plum tomatoes
⅓ cup tomato paste
1 cup water

½ teaspoon dried basil
¼ teaspoon dried oregano
Salt, pepper to taste
½ cup chopped fresh parsley
½ pound fresh mushrooms,
    cleaned & sliced

Heat the oil in a large skillet. Add the garlic and onion and sauté until tender. Mix in the tomatoes, tomato paste, water, basil, oregano, salt and pepper. Stir well and bring to a boil. Lower the heat and cook slowly, uncovered, for 1 hour, stirring occasionally. Add the parsley and mushrooms during the last 10 minutes of cooking. Makes slightly more than 5 cups.

Curried Mushroom Mayonnaise

Serve with seafood or poultry, or combine with potatoes for a salad.

1 cup mayonnaise	1 tablespoon fresh lemon
1 cup chopped fresh	juice
mushrooms	1 tablespoon curry powder
	Salt, cayenne to taste

Combine the ingredients and mix well. Chill. Makes about 2 cups.

Mushroom Pan Gravy

Serve with hamburgers, steak, meat loaf or pasta.

1 jar (2½ ounces) sliced	1 cup beef bouillon
mushrooms	Freshly grated nutmeg
2 tablespoons melted butter or	(optional)
margarine	Salt, pepper to taste
2 tablespoons flour	

Drain the mushrooms, reserving the liquid. Sauté the mushrooms in the butter for 5 minutes. Stir in the flour. Gradually add the mushroom liquid and bouillon. Cook slowly, stirring, until thickened and smooth. Season with nutmeg, salt and pepper. Makes about 1½ cups.

Creamy Mushroom Sauce

Serve with vegetables, fish, hard-cooked eggs or poultry.

½ pound fresh mushrooms
¼ cup butter or margarine
¼ cup flour

1 can (10½ ounces)
  condensed chicken broth
½ cup light cream
Salt, white pepper to taste

Clean and slice the mushrooms. Melt the butter in a saucepan. Add the mushrooms and sauté for 5 minutes. Stir in the flour. Gradually add the broth and cook slowly, stirring, until thickened and smooth. Stir in the cream, salt and pepper. Leave on the stove just long enough to heat through. Makes about 2 cups.

Sauce Chasseur

Serve with meat, poultry, game or pasta.

2 tablespoons butter or
  margarine
1 tablespoon olive or salad oil
2 tablespoons chopped shallots
  or green onions
2 tablespoons tomato paste

½ cup dry white wine
1 cup espagnole (brown
  sauce)
Salt, pepper to taste
1 teaspoon chopped fresh
  parsley

½ *pound fresh mushrooms,*   ½ *teaspoon chopped fresh*
  cleaned & sliced   *tarragon*

Melt the butter in a skillet. Add the oil and shallots, and sauté until they are tender. Add the sliced mushrooms and sauté for 4 minutes. Stir in the tomato paste. Add the wine, *espagnole* or brown sauce, salt and pepper. Cook slowly, stirring occasionally, for 10 minutes. Stir in the parsley and tarragon and remove from the heat. Makes a little more than 2 cups.

Herbed Mushroom Sauce

Serve with meat, poultry or game.

½ *pound fresh mushrooms,*   ½ *cup dry white wine*
  cleaned & sliced   2 *teaspoons chopped fresh*
¼ *cup butter or margarine*   *parsley*
2 *teaspoons lemon juice*   ¼ *teaspoon dried basil*
3 *tablespoons flour*   ¼ *teaspoon dried rosemary*
2 *cups chicken broth*   *Salt, pepper to taste*

Sauté the mushrooms in 2 tablespoons of butter and the lemon juice for 4 minutes and set aside. Melt the remaining 2 tablespoons of butter in a saucepan. Stir in the flour and cook, stirring, 1 minute. Gradually add the broth and cook slowly, stirring, until thickened and smooth. Add the wine, parsley, basil, rosemary, salt and pepper and continue to cook another 5 minutes. Makes about 3½ cups.

Mushroom Barbecue Sauce

Serve with grilled meat or poultry.

1 can (8 ounces) tomato
    sauce
1 can (6 ounces) tomato
    paste
1 cup ketchup
3 tablespoons brown sugar
2 teaspoons prepared mustard

2 tablespoons soy sauce
1 tablespoon vinegar
1½ teaspoons Worcestershire
    sauce
1 jar (4½ ounces) sliced
    mushrooms, undrained
Salt, pepper to taste

Combine the ingredients in a saucepan. Cook slowly, uncovered, for 20 minutes, stirring occasionally. Makes about 3½ cups.

Polish Fresh Mushroom Sauce

Serve with poultry, meat or game.

1 small onion, minced
¼ cup butter or margarine
2 cups sliced fresh mushrooms
1 tablespoon lemon juice
Salt, pepper to taste
2 tablespoons flour

1 cup beef bouillon
½ cup sour cream at room
    temperature
2 tablespoons minced dill or
    parsley

Sauté the onion in the butter in a saucepan until tender. Add the mushrooms and lemon juice, and sauté for 4 minutes. Season with salt and pepper. Stir in the flour and mix well.

Gradually add the bouillon and cook slowly, stirring, until thickened and smooth. Add the sour cream and dill and leave on the stove just long enough to heat through. Makes about 2 cups.

Sauce Bourguignonne

Serve with meat or poultry.

½ pound fresh mushrooms
2 tablespoons butter or
    margarine
2 teaspoons lemon juice
¼ cup minced cooked ham
⅓ cup minced carrot
⅓ cup finely chopped onion
1 garlic clove, crushed

1 tablespoon olive or salad oil
¼ teaspoon dried thyme
1 small bay leaf
1 cup dry red or white wine
Salt, pepper to taste
2 tablespoons chopped fresh
    parsley

Clean the mushrooms and cut into halves from the caps through the stems. Sauté in the butter and lemon juice for 4 minutes. Remove from the heat and set aside. Combine the ham, carrot, onion, garlic and oil in a skillet. Sauté the vegetables for 5 minutes. Add the thyme, bay leaf, wine, salt and pepper. Bring to a boil. Lower the heat and cook, uncovered, for 15 minutes. Add the sautéed mushrooms and parsley. Leave on the stove to heat through. Makes about 2 cups.

Mushroom Essence

This liquid, achieved by boiling down mushroom juices, may be kept in the refrigerator and used as needed to flavor soups, scrambled eggs, sauces, gravies or vegetables. It may be made as directed in this recipe or by reducing by one half the juices drained from canned mushrooms.

2 cups minced mushroom   1 tablespoon lemon juice
    stems   Salt, pepper to taste
2 cups beef bouillon, chicken
    broth or water

Combine the ingredients in a saucepan. Bring to a boil. Lower the heat a little and cook, uncovered, until the liquid is reduced by one half and becomes a little syrupy. Strain, pressing the mushrooms to extract all the juices. Pour into a bottle and keep tightly covered in the refrigerator.

Chicken Mushroom-Bread Stuffing

Use for a 4 to 5 pound chicken.

½ cup butter   ½ teaspoon poultry seasoning
½ cup chopped onion   1 teaspoon salt
1 cup sliced mushrooms, fresh   ⅛ teaspoon pepper
    or canned   ⅓ cup milk (optional)
4 cups stale bread cubes

Melt the butter in a skillet. Add the onion and sauté until tender. Add the mushrooms and sauté for 4 minutes. Remove from the heat and toss with the remaining ingredients.

Central European Noodle-Mushroom Stuffing

Use for a 5 to 6 pound chicken or turkey.

¼ cup butter or margarine
1 medium onion, chopped
1 cup chopped mushrooms,
   fresh or canned
8 ounces medium noodles,
   cooked & drained

½ cup milk
2 tablespoons chopped dill or
   ¼ cup chopped parsley
Salt, pepper to taste

Melt the butter in a skillet. Add the onion and sauté until tender. Add the mushrooms and sauté for 5 minutes. Remove from the heat and mix with the remaining ingredients.

Herbed Mushroom Stuffing

Use for a 10 to 12 pound turkey.

1 pound fresh mushrooms
½ cup butter or margarine
1½ cups chopped celery
1 cup chopped onion
1 package (7 ounces)
   seasoned bread crumbs

½ cup chicken broth
1 tablespoon chopped parsley
1 egg, lightly beaten
Salt, pepper to taste

Clean and slice the mushrooms. Melt the butter in a skillet. Add the celery and onion and sauté until the onions are tender. Add the mushrooms and sauté for 4 minutes. Remove from the heat and toss with the remaining ingredients.

Mushroom-Nut Stuffing

Use for a 12 to 16 pound turkey.

⅔ cup butter or margarine
1 cup chopped onion
½ cup chopped celery
1⅓ cups chopped mushrooms
12 cups stale bread cubes

1½ cups chopped nuts
  (pecans, Brazil, almonds,
  walnuts)
2 teaspoons poultry seasoning
Salt, pepper to taste

Melt the butter in a skillet. Add the onion and celery and sauté until the onions are tender. Add the mushrooms and sauté for 5 minutes. Remove from the heat and toss with the remaining ingredients.

Cornbread-Mushroom Stuffing

Use for a 6 to 8 pound capon or turkey.

4 slices bacon, cut into
  1-inch pieces
2 tablespoons butter or
  margarine
½ cup minced onion
1 cup sliced mushrooms,
  fresh or canned

3 cups stale bread cubes
4 cups crumbled unsweetened
  cornbread
1 egg, slightly beaten
¼ teaspoon dried thyme
¼ teaspoon ground sage

Cook the bacon until crisp. Remove from the heat and drain, reserving 2 tablespoons of fat. Put the fat and butter in a skillet. Add the onion and sauté until tender. Add the mushrooms and sauté for 4 minutes. Remove from the heat and mix with the bacon and the remaining ingredients.

Sherried Wild Rice-Mushroom Stuffing

Use for chicken or duckling.

1 medium onion, chopped
3 tablespoons butter
1 tablespoon lemon juice
½ pound fresh mushrooms,
    cleaned & sliced

1½ cups cooked wild rice
2 tablespoons orange juice
2 tablespoons dry sherry
½ teaspoon dried rosemary
Salt, pepper to taste

Sauté the onion in the butter in a saucepan until tender. Add the lemon juice and mushrooms and sauté for 4 minutes. Add the cooked rice, orange juice, sherry, rosemary, salt and pepper and cook 1 minute. Makes about 3 cups.

Oyster-Mushroom Stuffing

Use for a 4 to 5 pound fish or a 4 to 5 pound chicken.

1 pint oysters
½ cup butter or margarine
¼ cup chopped onion
¾ cup chopped mushrooms,
    fresh or canned

4 cups stale bread cubes
⅛ teaspoon poultry seasoning
2 tablespoons chopped fresh
    parsley
Salt, pepper to taste

Cook the oysters in their own liquid until the edges curl, only a few minutes. Drain and chop. Heat the butter in a skillet. Add the onion and sauté until tender. Add the mushrooms and sauté 4 minutes. Remove from the heat and mix with the chopped oysters and remaining ingredients.

Sausage-Mushroom Stuffing

Use for an 8 to 12 pound turkey.

1 pound pork sausage meat
½ cup chopped onion
1 cup chopped mushrooms,
    fresh or canned
½ cup milk

1 can (10½ ounces)
    condensed cream of
    mushroom soup
1 teaspoon dried thyme
2 tablespoons chopped fresh
    parsley
Salt, pepper to taste

Cook the sausage until the redness disappears. Pour off the fat, reserving ⅓ cup of it. Mince the sausage with a fork and set aside. Sauté the onion in the reserved fat until tender. Add the mushrooms and sauté 4 minutes. Stir in the milk and soup and mix well. Remove from the heat and mix with the sausage and the remaining ingredients.

Duckling Apple-Mushroom Stuffing

Use for a 4 to 5 pound duckling.

2 tablespoons minced onion
2 tablespoons butter
½ cup chopped mushrooms,
    fresh or canned
2½ cups stale bread cubes

1 cup peeled, chopped tart
    apples
⅓ cup apple juice
1 teasoon grated orange rind
Salt, pepper to taste

Sauté the onion in the butter until tender. Add the mushrooms and sauté 4 minutes. Mix with the remaining ingredients.

German Sauerkraut-Mushroom Stuffing

A good stuffing for a 10 to 12 pound goose.

1 ounce dried mushrooms
3 tablespoons butter or
    margarine, melted
1 medium onion, chopped

6 cups drained sauerkraut
2 teaspoons caraway seed
Salt, pepper to taste

Soak the mushrooms in lukewarm water to cover for 20 minutes. Drain, pressing to extract all the water. Slice. Combine with the remaining ingredients and mix well.

Mushroom Stuffing for Fish

Use for a 3 to 4 pound dressed fish or for stuffing 2 fish fillets, about 1 pound each.

¼ cup chopped green onions,
    with tops
¼ cup chopped celery
6 tablespoons butter or
    margarine
1 cup chopped mushrooms,
    fresh or canned

4 cups stale bread cubes
1 teaspoon dried herbs
    (thyme, basil, marjoram,
    rosemary)
2 tablespoons milk
Salt, pepper to taste

Sauté the onions and celery in the butter until tender. Add the mushrooms and sauté for 5 minutes. Mix with the remaining ingredients.

Cape Cod Mushroom-Clam Stuffing

Use for 3 to 4 pound fish, green peppers or tomatoes.

1 can (about 5 ounces)
   minced clams
3 tablespoons minced onion
3 tablespoons minced celery
1/4 cup butter or margarine

1/2 cup chopped mushrooms,
   fresh or canned
1 1/2 cups stale bread cubes
1/2 teaspoon dried thyme
Salt, pepper to taste

Drain the clams, reserving the liquid. Sauté the onion and celery in the butter until the onions are tender. Add the mushrooms and sauté 4 minutes. Remove from the heat and mix with the remaining ingredients.

Mushroom-Rice Stuffing

Use for stuffing fish, poultry or tomatoes.

1/4 cup butter or margarine
1 medium onion, chopped
1/2 cup chopped celery
1/4 pound fresh mushrooms,
   cleaned & sliced

2 1/2 cups cold cooked rice
2 tablespoons chopped dill
Salt, pepper to taste

Melt the butter in a skillet. Add the onion and celery and sauté until the onions are tender. Add the mushrooms and sauté for 4 minutes. Mix with the remaining ingredients. Makes about 4 cups.

Index

SALADS AND VEGETABLES   187-201

SAUCES AND STUFFINGS   203-220

SEAFOOD   117-137

SOUPS   49-71

A CATALOGUE OF
SELECTED DOVER BOOKS
IN ALL FIELDS OF INTEREST

A CATALOGUE OF SELECTED DOVER
BOOKS IN ALL FIELDS OF INTEREST

RACKHAM'S COLOR ILLUSTRATIONS FOR WAGNER'S RING. Rackham's finest mature work—all 64 full-color watercolors in a faithful and lush interpretation of the *Ring*. Full-sized plates on coated stock of the paintings used by opera companies for authentic staging of Wagner. Captions aid in following complete Ring cycle. Introduction. 64 illustrations plus vignettes. 72pp. 8⅝ x 11¼. 23779-6 Pa. $6.00

CONTEMPORARY POLISH POSTERS IN FULL COLOR, edited by Joseph Czestochowski. 46 full-color examples of brilliant school of Polish graphic design, selected from world's first museum (near Warsaw) dedicated to poster art. Posters on circuses, films, plays, concerts all show cosmopolitan influences, free imagination. Introduction. 48pp. 9⅜ x 12¼. 23780-X Pa. $6.00

GRAPHIC WORKS OF EDVARD MUNCH, Edvard Munch. 90 haunting, evocative prints by first major Expressionist artist and one of the greatest graphic artists of his time: *The Scream, Anxiety, Death Chamber, The Kiss, Madonna,* etc. Introduction by Alfred Werner. 90pp. 9 x 12. 23765-6 Pa. $5.00

THE GOLDEN AGE OF THE POSTER, Hayward and Blanche Cirker. 70 extraordinary posters in full colors, from Maitres de l'Affiche, Mucha, Lautrec, Bradley, Cheret, Beardsley, many others. Total of 78pp. 9⅜ x 12¼. 22753-7 Pa. $5.95

THE NOTEBOOKS OF LEONARDO DA VINCI, edited by J. P. Richter. Extracts from manuscripts reveal great genius; on painting, sculpture, anatomy, sciences, geography, etc. Both Italian and English. 186 ms. pages reproduced, plus 500 additional drawings, including studies for *Last Supper,* Sforza monument, etc. 860pp. 7⅞ x 10¾. (Available in U.S. only) 22572-0, 22573-9 Pa., Two-vol. set $15.90

THE CODEX NUTTALL, as first edited by Zelia Nuttall. Only inexpensive edition, in full color, of a pre-Columbian Mexican (Mixtec) book. 88 color plates show kings, gods, heroes, temples, sacrifices. New explanatory, historical introduction by Arthur G. Miller. 96pp. 11⅜ x 8½. (Available in U.S. only) 23168-2 Pa. $7.95

UNE SEMAINE DE BONTÉ, A SURREALISTIC NOVEL IN COLLAGE, Max Ernst. Masterpiece created out of 19th-century periodical illustrations, explores worlds of terror and surprise. Some consider this Ernst's greatest work. 208pp. 8⅛ x 11. 23252-2 Pa. $6.00

DRAWINGS OF WILLIAM BLAKE, William Blake. 92 plates from Book of Job, *Divine Comedy, Paradise Lost,* visionary heads, mythological figures, Laocoon, etc. Selection, introduction, commentary by Sir Geoffrey Keynes. 178pp. 8⅛ x 11.   22303-5 Pa. $4.00

ENGRAVINGS OF HOGARTH, William Hogarth. 101 of Hogarth's greatest works: *Rake's Progress, Harlot's Progress, Illustrations for Hudibras, Before and After, Beer Street and Gin Lane,* many more. Full commentary. 256pp. 11 x 13¾.   22479-1 Pa. $12.95

DAUMIER: 120 GREAT LITHOGRAPHS, Honore Daumier. Wide-ranging collection of lithographs by the greatest caricaturist of the 19th century. Concentrates on eternally popular series on lawyers, on married life, on liberated women, etc. Selection, introduction, and notes on plates by Charles F. Ramus. Total of 158pp. 9⅜ x 12¼.   23512-2 Pa. $6.00

DRAWINGS OF MUCHA, Alphonse Maria Mucha. Work reveals drafts-man of highest caliber: studies for famous posters and paintings, render-ings for book illustrations and ads, etc. 70 works, 9 in color; including 6 items not drawings. Introduction. List of illustrations. 72pp. 9⅜ x 12¼. (Available in U.S. only)   23672-2 Pa. $4.00

GIOVANNI BATTISTA PIRANESI: DRAWINGS IN THE PIERPONT MORGAN LIBRARY, Giovanni Battista Piranesi. For first time ever all of Morgan Library's collection, world's largest. 167 illustrations of rare Piranesi drawings—archeological, architectural, decorative and visionary. Essay, detailed list of drawings, chronology, captions. Edited by Felice Stampfle. 144pp. 9⅜ x 12¼.   23714-1 Pa. $7.50

NEW YORK ETCHINGS (1905-1949), John Sloan. All of important American artist's N.Y. life etchings. 67 works include some of his best art; also lively historical record—Greenwich Village, tenement scenes. Edited by Sloan's widow. Introduction and captions. 79pp. 8⅜ x 11¼. 23651-X Pa. $4.00

CHINESE PAINTING AND CALLIGRAPHY: A PICTORIAL SURVEY, Wan-go Weng. 69 fine examples from John M. Crawford's matchless private collection: landscapes, birds, flowers, human figures, etc., plus calligraphy. Every basic form included: hanging scrolls, handscrolls, album leaves, fans, etc. 109 illustrations. Introduction. Captions. 192pp. 8⅞ x 11¾. 23707-9 Pa. $7.95

DRAWINGS OF REMBRANDT, edited by Seymour Slive. Updated Lipp-mann, Hofstede de Groot edition, with definitive scholarly apparatus. All portraits, biblical sketches, landscapes, nudes, Oriental figures, classical studies, together with selection of work by followers. 550 illustrations. Total of 630pp. 9⅛ x 12¼.   21485-0, 21486-9 Pa., Two-vol. set $15.00

THE DISASTERS OF WAR, Francisco Goya. 83 etchings record horrors of Napoleonic wars in Spain and war in general. Reprint of 1st edition, plus 3 additional plates. Introduction by Philip Hofer. 97pp. 9⅜ x 8¼. 21872-4 Pa. $4.00

THE EARLY WORK OF AUBREY BEARDSLEY, Aubrey Beardsley. 157 plates, 2 in color: *Manon Lescaut, Madame Bovary, Morte Darthur, Salome,* other. Introduction by H. Marillier. 182pp. 8⅛ x 11. 21816-3 Pa. $4.50

THE LATER WORK OF AUBREY BEARDSLEY, Aubrey Beardsley. Exotic masterpieces of full maturity: *Venus and Tannhauser, Lysistrata, Rape of the Lock, Volpone,* Savoy material, etc. 174 plates, 2 in color. 186pp. 8⅛ x 11. 21817-1 Pa. $5.95

THOMAS NAST'S CHRISTMAS DRAWINGS, Thomas Nast. Almost all Christmas drawings by creator of image of Santa Claus as we know it, and one of America's foremost illustrators and political cartoonists. 66 illustrations. 3 illustrations in color on covers. 96pp. 8⅜ x 11¼. 23660-9 Pa. $3.50

THE DORÉ ILLUSTRATIONS FOR DANTE'S DIVINE COMEDY, Gustave Doré. All 135 plates from Inferno, Purgatory, Paradise; fantastic tortures, infernal landscapes, celestial wonders. Each plate with appropriate (translated) verses. 141pp. 9 x 12. 23231-X Pa. $4.50

DORÉ'S ILLUSTRATIONS FOR RABELAIS, Gustave Doré. 252 striking illustrations of *Gargantua and Pantagruel* books by foremost 19th-century illustrator. Including 60 plates, 192 delightful smaller illustrations. 153pp. 9 x 12. 23656-0 Pa. $5.00

LONDON: A PILGRIMAGE, Gustave Doré, Blanchard Jerrold. Squalor, riches, misery, beauty of mid-Victorian metropolis; 55 wonderful plates, 125 other illustrations, full social, cultural text by Jerrold. 191pp. of text. 9⅜ x 12¼. 22306-X Pa. $7.00

THE RIME OF THE ANCIENT MARINER, Gustave Doré, S. T. Coleridge. Dore's finest work, 34 plates capture moods, subtleties of poem. Full text. Introduction by Millicent Rose. 77pp. 9¼ x 12. 22305-1 Pa. $3.50

THE DORE BIBLE ILLUSTRATIONS, Gustave Doré. All wonderful, detailed plates: Adam and Eve, Flood, Babylon, Life of Jesus, etc. Brief King James text with each plate. Introduction by Millicent Rose. 241 plates. 241pp. 9 x 12. 23004-X Pa. $6.00

THE COMPLETE ENGRAVINGS, ETCHINGS AND DRYPOINTS OF ALBRECHT DURER. "Knight, Death and Devil"; "Melencolia," and more—all Dürer's known works in all three media, including 6 works formerly attributed to him. 120 plates. 235pp. 8⅜ x 11¼. 22851-7 Pa. $6.50

MECHANICK EXERCISES ON THE WHOLE ART OF PRINTING, Joseph Moxon. First complete book (1683-4) ever written about typography, a compendium of everything known about printing at the latter part of 17th century. Reprint of 2nd (1962) Oxford Univ. Press edition. 74 illustrations. Total of 550pp. 6⅛ x 9¼. 23617-X Pa. $7.95

THE COMPLETE WOODCUTS OF ALBRECHT DURER, edited by Dr. W. Kurth. 346 in all: "Old Testament," "St. Jerome," "Passion," "Life of Virgin," "Apocalypse," many others. Introduction by Campbell Dodgson. 285pp. 8½ x 12¼. 21097-9 Pa. $7.50

DRAWINGS OF ALBRECHT DURER, edited by Heinrich Wolfflin. 81 plates show development from youth to full style. Many favorites; many new. Introduction by Alfred Werner. 96pp. 8⅛ x 11. 22352-3 Pa. $5.00

THE HUMAN FIGURE, Albrecht Dürer. Experiments in various techniques—stereometric, progressive proportional, and others. Also life studies that rank among finest ever done. Complete reprinting of *Dresden Sketchbook*. 170 plates. 355pp. 8⅜ x 11¼. 21042-1 Pa. $7.95

OF THE JUST SHAPING OF LETTERS, Albrecht Dürer. Renaissance artist explains design of Roman majuscules by geometry, also Gothic lower and capitals. Grolier Club edition. 43pp. 7⅞ x 10¾ 21306-4 Pa. $3.00

TEN BOOKS ON ARCHITECTURE, Vitruvius. The most important book ever written on architecture. Early Roman aesthetics, technology, classical orders, site selection, all other aspects. Stands behind everything since. Morgan translation. 331pp. 5⅜ x 8½. 20645-9 Pa. $4.50

THE FOUR BOOKS OF ARCHITECTURE, Andrea Palladio. 16th-century classic responsible for Palladian movement and style. Covers classical architectural remains, Renaissance revivals, classical orders, etc. 1738 Ware English edition. Introduction by A. Placzek. 216 plates. 110pp. of text. 9½ x 12¾. 21308-0 Pa. $10.00

HORIZONS, Norman Bel Geddes. Great industrialist stage designer, "father of streamlining," on application of aesthetics to transportation, amusement, architecture, etc. 1932 prophetic account; function, theory, specific projects. 222 illustrations. 312pp. 7⅞ x 10¾. 23514-9 Pa. $6.95

FRANK LLOYD WRIGHT'S FALLINGWATER, Donald Hoffmann. Full, illustrated story of conception and building of Wright's masterwork at Bear Run, Pa. 100 photographs of site, construction, and details of completed structure. 112pp. 9¼ x 10. 23671-4 Pa. $5.50

THE ELEMENTS OF DRAWING, John Ruskin. Timeless classic by great Viltorian; starts with basic ideas, works through more difficult. Many practical exercises. 48 illustrations. Introduction by Lawrence Campbell. 228pp. 5⅜ x 8½. 22730-8 Pa. $3.75

GIST OF ART, John Sloan. Greatest modern American teacher, Art Students League, offers innumerable hints, instructions, guided comments to help you in painting. Not a formal course. 46 illustrations. Introduction by Helen Sloan. 200pp. 5⅜ x 8½. 23435-5 Pa. $4.00

THE ANATOMY OF THE HORSE, George Stubbs. Often considered the great masterpiece of animal anatomy. Full reproduction of 1766 edition, plus prospectus; original text and modernized text. 36 plates. Introduction by Eleanor Garvey. 121pp. 11 x 14¾.   23402-9 Pa. $6.00

BRIDGMAN'S LIFE DRAWING, George B. Bridgman. More than 500 illustrative drawings and text teach you to abstract the body into its major masses, use light and shade, proportion; as well as specific areas of anatomy, of which Bridgman is master. 192pp. 6½ x 9¼. (Available in U.S. only)
22710-3 Pa. $3.50

ART NOUVEAU DESIGNS IN COLOR, Alphonse Mucha, Maurice Verneuil, Georges Auriol. Full-color reproduction of *Combinaisons ornementales* (c. 1900) by Art Nouveau masters. Floral, animal, geometric, interlacings, swashes—borders, frames, spots—all incredibly beautiful. 60 plates, hundreds of designs. 9⅜ x 8-1/16.   22885-1 Pa. $4.00

FULL-COLOR FLORAL DESIGNS IN THE ART NOUVEAU STYLE, E. A. Seguy. 166 motifs, on 40 plates, from *Les fleurs et leurs applications decoratives* (1902): borders, circular designs, repeats, allovers, "spots." All in authentic Art Nouveau colors. 48pp. 9⅜ x 12¼.
23439-8 Pa. $5.00

A DIDEROT PICTORIAL ENCYCLOPEDIA OF TRADES AND INDUSTRY, edited by Charles C. Gillispie. 485 most interesting plates from the great French Encyclopedia of the 18th century show hundreds of working figures, artifacts, process, land and cityscapes; glassmaking, papermaking, metal extraction, construction, weaving, making furniture, clothing, wigs, dozens of other activities. Plates fully explained. 920pp. 9 x 12.
22284-5, 22285-3 Clothbd., Two-vol. set $40.00

HANDBOOK OF EARLY ADVERTISING ART, Clarence P. Hornung. Largest collection of copyright-free early and antique advertising art ever compiled. Over 6,000 illustrations, from Franklin's time to the 1890's for special effects, novelty. Valuable source, almost inexhaustible.
Pictorial Volume. Agriculture, the zodiac, animals, autos, birds, Christmas, fire engines, flowers, trees, musical instruments, ships, games and sports, much more. Arranged by subject matter and use. 237 plates. 288pp. 9 x 12.
20122-8 Clothbd. $14.50

Typographical Volume. Roman and Gothic faces ranging from 10 point to 300 point, "Barnum," German and Old English faces, script, logotypes, scrolls and flourishes, 1115 ornamental initials, 67 complete alphabets, more. 310 plates. 320pp. 9 x 12.   20123-6 Clothbd. $15.00

CALLIGRAPHY (CALLIGRAPHIA LATINA), J. G. Schwandner. High point of 18th-century ornamental calligraphy. Very ornate initials, scrolls, borders, cherubs, birds, lettered examples. 172pp. 9 x 13.
20475-8 Pa. $7.00

ART FORMS IN NATURE, Ernst Haeckel. Multitude of strangely beautiful natural forms: Radiolaria, Foraminifera, jellyfishes, fungi, turtles, bats, etc. All 100 plates of the 19th-century evolutionist's *Kunstformen der Natur* (1904). 100pp. 9⅜ x 12¼. 22987-4 Pa. $5.00

CHILDREN: A PICTORIAL ARCHIVE FROM NINETEENTH-CENTURY SOURCES, edited by Carol Belanger Grafton. 242 rare, copyright-free wood engravings for artists and designers. Widest such selection available. All illustrations in line. 119pp. 8⅜ x 11¼. 23694-3 Pa. $4.00

WOMEN: A PICTORIAL ARCHIVE FROM NINETEENTH-CENTURY SOURCES, edited by Jim Harter. 391 copyright-free wood engravings for artists and designers selected from rare periodicals. Most extensive such collection available. All illustrations in line. 128pp. 9 x 12. 23703-6 Pa. $4.50

ARABIC ART IN COLOR, Prisse d'Avennes. From the greatest ornamentalists of all time—50 plates in color, rarely seen outside the Near East, rich in suggestion and stimulus. Includes 4 plates on covers. 46pp. 9⅜ x 12¼. 23658-7 Pa. $6.00

AUTHENTIC ALGERIAN CARPET DESIGNS AND MOTIFS, edited by June Beveridge. Algerian carpets are world famous. Dozens of geometrical motifs are charted on grids, color-coded, for weavers, needleworkers, craftsmen, designers. 53 illustrations plus 4 in color. 48pp. 8¼ x 11. (Available in U.S. only) 23650-1 Pa. $1.75

DICTIONARY OF AMERICAN PORTRAITS, edited by Hayward and Blanche Cirker. 4000 important Americans, earliest times to 1905, mostly in clear line. Politicians, writers, soldiers, scientists, inventors, industrialists, Indians, Blacks, women, outlaws, etc. Identificatory information. 756pp. 9¼ x 12¾. 21823-6 Clothbd. $40.00

HOW THE OTHER HALF LIVES, Jacob A. Riis. Journalistic record of filth, degradation, upward drive in New York immigrant slums, shops, around 1900. New edition includes 100 original Riis photos, monuments of early photography. 233pp. 10 x 7⅞. 22012-5 Pa. $7.00

NEW YORK IN THE THIRTIES, Berenice Abbott. Noted photographer's fascinating study of city shows new buildings that have become famous and old sights that have disappeared forever. Insightful commentary. 97 photographs. 97pp. 11⅜ x 10. 22967-X Pa. $5.00

MEN AT WORK, Lewis W. Hine. Famous photographic studies of construction workers, railroad men, factory workers and coal miners. New supplement of 18 photos on Empire State building construction. New introduction by Jonathan L. Doherty. Total of 69 photos. 63pp. 8 x 10¾. 23475-4 Pa. $3.00

THE DEPRESSION YEARS AS PHOTOGRAPHED BY ARTHUR ROTH-STEIN, Arthur Rothstein. First collection devoted entirely to the work of outstanding 1930s photographer: famous dust storm photo, ragged children, unemployed, etc. 120 photographs. Captions. 119pp. 9¼ x 10¾.
23590-4 Pa. $5.00

CAMERA WORK: A PICTORIAL GUIDE, Alfred Stieglitz. All 559 illustrations and plates from the most important periodical in the history of art photography, Camera Work (1903-17). Presented four to a page, reduced in size but still clear, in strict chronological order, with complete captions. Three indexes. Glossary. Bibliography. 176pp. 8⅜ x 11¼.
23591-2 Pa. $6.95

ALVIN LANGDON COBURN, PHOTOGRAPHER, Alvin L. Coburn. Revealing autobiography by one of greatest photographers of 20th century gives insider's version of Photo-Secession, plus comments on his own work. 77 photographs by Coburn. Edited by Helmut and Alison Gernsheim. 160pp. 8⅛ x 11.
23685-4 Pa. $6.00

NEW YORK IN THE FORTIES, Andreas Feininger. 162 brilliant photographs by the well-known photographer, formerly with Life magazine, show commuters, shoppers, Times Square at night, Harlem nightclub, Lower East Side, etc. Introduction and full captions by John von Hartz. 181pp. 9¼ x 10¾.
23585-8 Pa. $6.95

GREAT NEWS PHOTOS AND THE STORIES BEHIND THEM, John Faber. Dramatic volume of 140 great news photos, 1855 through 1976, and revealing stories behind them, with both historical and technical information. Hindenburg disaster, shooting of Oswald, nomination of Jimmy Carter, etc. 160pp. 8¼ x 11.
23667-6 Pa. $5.00

THE ART OF THE CINEMATOGRAPHER, Leonard Maltin. Survey of American cinematography history and anecdotal interviews with 5 masters—Arthur Miller, Hal Mohr, Hal Rosson, Lucien Ballard, and Conrad Hall. Very large selection of behind-the-scenes production photos. 105 photographs. Filmographies. Index. Originally Behind the Camera. 144pp. 8¼ x 11.
23686-2 Pa. $5.00

DESIGNS FOR THE THREE-CORNERED HAT (LE TRICORNE), Pablo Picasso. 32 fabulously rare drawings—including 31 color illustrations of costumes and accessories—for 1919 production of famous ballet. Edited by Parmenia Migel, who has written new introduction. 48pp. 9⅜ x 12¼. (Available in U.S. only)
23709-5 Pa. $5.00

NOTES OF A FILM DIRECTOR, Sergei Eisenstein. Greatest Russian filmmaker explains montage, making of Alexander Nevsky, aesthetics; comments on self, associates, great rivals (Chaplin), similar material. 78 illustrations. 240pp. 5⅜ x 8½.
22392-2 Pa. $4.50

HOLLYWOOD GLAMOUR PORTRAITS, edited by John Kobal. 145 photos capture the stars from 1926-49, the high point in portrait photography. Gable, Harlow, Bogart, Bacall, Hedy Lamarr, Marlene Dietrich, Robert Montgomery, Marlon Brando, Veronica Lake; 94 stars in all. Full background on photographers, technical aspects, much more. Total of 160pp. 8⅜ x 11¼. 23352-9 Pa. $6.00

THE NEW YORK STAGE: FAMOUS PRODUCTIONS IN PHOTO-GRAPHS, edited by Stanley Appelbaum. 148 photographs from Museum of City of New York show 142 plays, 1883-1939. *Peter Pan, The Front Page, Dead End, Our Town,* O'Neill, hundreds of actors and actresses, etc. Full indexes. 154pp. 9½ x 10. 23241-7 Pa. $6.00

DIALOGUES CONCERNING TWO NEW SCIENCES, Galileo Galilei. Encompassing 30 years of experiment and thought, these dialogues deal with geometric demonstrations of fracture of solid bodies, cohesion, leverage, speed of light and sound, pendulums, falling bodies, accelerated motion, etc. 300pp. 5⅜ x 8½. 60099-8 Pa. $4.00

THE GREAT OPERA STARS IN HISTORIC PHOTOGRAPHS, edited by James Camner. 343 portraits from the 1850s to the 1940s: Tamburini, Mario, Caliapin, Jeritza, Melchior, Melba, Patti, Pinza, Schipa, Caruso, Farrar, Steber, Gobbi, and many more—270 performers in all. Index. 199pp. 8⅜ x 11¼. 23575-0 Pa. $7.50

J. S. BACH, Albert Schweitzer. Great full-length study of Bach, life, background to music, music, by foremost modern scholar. Ernest Newman translation. 650 musical examples. Total of 928pp. 5⅜ x 8½. (Available in U.S. only) 21631-4, 21632-2 Pa., Two-vol. set $11.00

COMPLETE PIANO SONATAS, Ludwig van Beethoven. All sonatas in the fine Schenker edition, with fingering, analytical material. One of best modern editions. Total of 615pp. 9 x 12. (Available in U.S. only)
23134-8, 23135-6 Pa., Two-vol. set $15.50

KEYBOARD MUSIC, J. S. Bach. Bach-Gesellschaft edition. For harpsichord, piano, other keyboard instruments. English Suites, French Suites, Six Partitas, Goldberg Variations, Two-Part Inventions, Three-Part Sinfonias. 312pp. 8⅛ x 11. (Available in U.S. only) 22360-4 Pa. $6.95

FOUR SYMPHONIES IN FULL SCORE, Franz Schubert. Schubert's four most popular symphonies: No. 4 in C Minor ("Tragic"); No. 5 in B-flat Major; No. 8 in B Minor ("Unfinished"); No. 9 in C Major ("Great"). Breitkopf & Hartel edition. Study score. 261pp. 9⅜ x 12¼.
23681-1 Pa. $6.50

THE AUTHENTIC GILBERT & SULLIVAN SONGBOOK, W. S. Gilbert, A. S. Sullivan. Largest selection available; 92 songs, uncut, original keys, in piano rendering approved by Sullivan. Favorites and lesser-known fine numbers. Edited with plot synopses by James Spero. 3 illustrations. 399pp. 9 x 12. 23482-7 Pa. $9.95

PRINCIPLES OF ORCHESTRATION, Nikolay Rimsky-Korsakov. Great classical orchestrator provides fundamentals of tonal resonance, progression of parts, voice and orchestra, tutti effects, much else in major document. 330pp. of musical excerpts. 489pp. 6½ x 9¼.   21266-1 Pa. **$7.50**

TRISTAN UND ISOLDE, Richard Wagner. Full orchestral score with complete instrumentation. Do not confuse with piano reduction. Commentary by Felix Mottl, great Wagnerian conductor and scholar. Study score. 655pp. 8⅛ x 11.   22915-7 Pa. **$13.95**

REQUIEM IN FULL SCORE, Giuseppe Verdi. Immensely popular with choral groups and music lovers. Republication of edition published by C. F. Peters, Leipzig, n. d. German frontmaker in English translation. Glossary. Text in Latin. Study score. 204pp. 9⅜ x 12¼.

23682-X Pa. **$6.00**

COMPLETE CHAMBER MUSIC FOR STRINGS, Felix Mendelssohn. All of Mendelssohn's chamber music: Octet, 2 Quintets, 6 Quartets, and Four Pieces for String Quartet. (Nothing with piano is included). Complete works edition (1874-7). Study score. 283 pp. 9⅜ x 12¼.

23679-X Pa. **$7.50**

POPULAR SONGS OF NINETEENTH-CENTURY AMERICA, edited by Richard Jackson. 64 most important songs: "Old Oaken Bucket," "Arkansas Traveler," "Yellow Rose of Texas," etc. Authentic original sheet music, full introduction and commentaries. 290pp. 9 x 12.   23270-0 Pa. **$7.95**

COLLECTED PIANO WORKS, Scott Joplin. Edited by Vera Brodsky Lawrence. Practically all of Joplin's piano works—rags, two-steps, marches, waltzes, etc., 51 works in all. Extensive introduction by Rudi Blesh. Total of 345pp. 9 x 12.   23106-2 Pa. **$14.95**

BASIC PRINCIPLES OF CLASSICAL BALLET, Agrippina Vaganova. Great Russian theoretician, teacher explains methods for teaching classical ballet; incorporates best from French, Italian, Russian schools. 118 illustrations. 175pp. 5⅜ x 8½.   22036-2 Pa. **$2.50**

CHINESE CHARACTERS, L. Wieger. Rich analysis of 2300 characters according to traditional systems into primitives. Historical-semantic analysis to phonetics (Classical Mandarin) and radicals. 820pp. 6⅛ x 9¼.

21321-8 Pa. **$10.00**

EGYPTIAN LANGUAGE: EASY LESSONS IN EGYPTIAN HIERO-GLYPHICS, E. A. Wallis Budge. Foremost Egyptologist offers Egyptian grammar, explanation of hieroglyphics, many reading texts, dictionary of symbols. 246pp. 5 x 7½. (Available in U.S. only)

21394-3 Clothbd. **$7.50**

AN ETYMOLOGICAL DICTIONARY OF MODERN ENGLISH, Ernest Weekley. Richest, fullest work, by foremost British lexicographer. Detailed word histories. Inexhaustible. Do not confuse this with *Concise Etymological Dictionary*, which is abridged. Total of 856pp. 6½ x 9¼.

21873-2, 21874-0 Pa., Two-vol. set **$12.00**

A MAYA GRAMMAR, Alfred M. Tozzer. Practical, useful English-language grammar by the Harvard anthropologist who was one of the three greatest American scholars in the area of Maya culture. Phonetics, grammatical processes, syntax, more. 301pp. 5⅜ x 8½.   23465-7 Pa. $4.00

THE JOURNAL OF HENRY D. THOREAU, edited by Bradford Torrey, F. H. Allen. Complete reprinting of 14 volumes, 1837-61, over two million words; the sourcebooks for *Walden*, etc. Definitive. All original sketches, plus 75 photographs. Introduction by Walter Harding. Total of 1804pp. 8½ x 12¼.   20312-3, 20313-1 Clothbd., Two-vol. set $70.00

CLASSIC GHOST STORIES, Charles Dickens and others. 18 wonderful stories you've wanted to reread: "The Monkey's Paw," "The House and the Brain," "The Upper Berth," "The Signalman," "Dracula's Guest," "The Tapestried Chamber," etc. Dickens, Scott, Mary Shelley, Stoker, etc. 330pp. 5⅜ x 8½.   20735-8 Pa. $4.50

SEVEN SCIENCE FICTION NOVELS, H. G. Wells. Full novels. *First Men in the Moon, Island of Dr. Moreau, War of the Worlds, Food of the Gods, Invisible Man, Time Machine, In the Days of the Comet.* A basic science-fiction library. 1015pp. 5⅜ x 8½. (Available in U.S. only)
20264-X Clothbd. $8.95

ARMADALE, Wilkie Collins. Third great mystery novel by the author of *The Woman in White* and *The Moonstone*. Ingeniously plotted narrative shows an exceptional command of character, incident and mood. Original magazine version with 40 illustrations. 597pp. 5⅜ x 8½.
23429-0 Pa. $6.00

MASTERS OF MYSTERY, H. Douglas Thomson. The first book in English (1931) devoted to history and aesthetics of detective story. Poe, Doyle, LeFanu, Dickens, many others, up to 1930. New introduction and notes by E. F. Bleiler. 288pp. 5⅜ x 8½. (Available in U.S. only)
23606-4 Pa. $4.00

FLATLAND, E. A. Abbott. Science-fiction classic explores life of 2-D being in 3-D world. Read also as introduction to thought about hyperspace. Introduction by Banesh Hoffmann. 16 illustrations. 103pp. 5⅜ x 8½.
20001-9 Pa. $2.00

THREE SUPERNATURAL NOVELS OF THE VICTORIAN PERIOD, edited, with an introduction, by E. F. Bleiler. Reprinted complete and unabridged, three great classics of the supernatural: *The Haunted Hotel* by Wilkie Collins, *The Haunted House at Latchford* by Mrs. J. H. Riddell, and *The Lost Stradivarious* by J. Meade Falkner. 325pp. 5⅜ x 8½.
22571-2 Pa. $4.00

AYESHA: THE RETURN OF "SHE," H. Rider Haggard. Virtuoso sequel featuring the great mythic creation, Ayesha, in an adventure that is fully as good as the first book, *She*. Original magazine version, with 47 original illustrations by Maurice Greiffenhagen. 189pp. 6½ x 9¼.
23649-8 Pa. $3.50

UNCLE SILAS, J. Sheridan LeFanu. Victorian Gothic mystery novel, considered by many best of period, even better than Collins or Dickens. Wonderful psychological terror. Introduction by Frederick Shroyer. 436pp. 5⅜ x 8½.   21715-9 Pa. $6.00

JURGEN, James Branch Cabell. The great erotic fantasy of the 1920's that delighted thousands, shocked thousands more. Full final text, Lane edition with 13 plates by Frank Pape. 346pp. 5⅜ x 8½.
                                                                      23507-6 Pa. $4.50

THE CLAVERINGS, Anthony Trollope. Major novel, chronicling aspects of British Victorian society, personalities. Reprint of Cornhill serialization, 16 plates by M. Edwards; first reprint of full text. Introduction by Norman Donaldson. 412pp. 5⅜ x 8½.   23464-9 Pa. $5.00

KEPT IN THE DARK, Anthony Trollope. Unusual short novel about Victorian morality and abnormal psychology by the great English author. Probably the first American publication. Frontispiece by Sir John Millais. 92pp. 6½ x 9¼.   23609-9 Pa. $2.50

RALPH THE HEIR, Anthony Trollope. Forgotten tale of illegitimacy, inheritance. Master novel of Trollope's later years. Victorian country estates, clubs, Parliament, fox hunting, world of fully realized characters. Reprint of 1871 edition. 12 illustrations by F. A. Faser. 434pp. of text. 5⅜ x 8½.   23642-0 Pa. $5.00

YEKL and THE IMPORTED BRIDEGROOM AND OTHER STORIES OF THE NEW YORK GHETTO, Abraham Cahan. Film *Hester Street* based on *Yekl* (1896). Novel, other stories among first about Jewish immigrants of N.Y.'s East Side. Highly praised by W. D. Howells—Cahan "a new star of realism." New introduction by Bernard G. Richards. 240pp. 5⅜ x 8½.   22427-9 Pa. $3.50

THE HIGH PLACE, James Branch Cabell. Great fantasy writer's enchanting comedy of disenchantment set in 18th-century France. Considered by some critics to be even better than his famous *Jurgen*. 10 illustrations and numerous vignettes by noted fantasy artist Frank C. Pape. 320pp. 5⅜ x 8½.   23670-6 Pa. $4.00

ALICE'S ADVENTURES UNDER GROUND, Lewis Carroll. Facsimile of ms. Carroll gave Alice Liddell in 1864. Different in many ways from final Alice. Handlettered, illustrated by Carroll. Introduction by Martin Gardner. 128pp. 5⅜ x 8½.   21482-6 Pa. $2.50

FAVORITE ANDREW LANG FAIRY TALE BOOKS IN MANY COLORS, Andrew Lang. The four Lang favorites in a boxed set—the complete *Red, Green, Yellow* and *Blue* Fairy Books. 164 stories; 439 illustrations by Lancelot Speed, Henry Ford and G. P. Jacomb Hood. Total of about 1500pp. 5⅜ x 8½.   23407-X Boxed set, Pa. $15.95

HOUSEHOLD STORIES BY THE BROTHERS GRIMM. All the great Grimm stories: "Rumpelstiltskin," "Snow White," "Hansel and Gretel," etc., with 114 illustrations by Walter Crane. 269pp. 5⅜ x 8½.
21080-4 Pa. $3.50

SLEEPING BEAUTY, illustrated by Arthur Rackham. Perhaps the fullest, most delightful version ever, told by C. S. Evans. Rackham's best work. 49 illustrations. 110pp. 7⅞ x 10¾. 22756-1 Pa. $2.50

AMERICAN FAIRY TALES, L. Frank Baum. Young cowboy lassoes Father Time; dummy in Mr. Floman's department store window comes to life; and 10 other fairy tales. 41 illustrations by N. P. Hall, Harry Kennedy, Ike Morgan, and Ralph Gardner. 209pp. 5⅜ x 8½. 23643-9 Pa. $3.00

THE WONDERFUL WIZARD OF OZ, L. Frank Baum. Facsimile in full color of America's finest children's classic. Introduction by Martin Gardner. 143 illustrations by W. W. Denslow. 267pp. 5⅜ x 8½.
20691-2 Pa. $3.50

THE TALE OF PETER RABBIT, Beatrix Potter. The inimitable Peter's terrifying adventure in Mr. McGregor's garden, with all 27 wonderful, full-color Potter illustrations. 55pp. 4¼ x 5½. (Available in U.S. only)
22827-4 Pa. $1.25

THE STORY OF KING ARTHUR AND HIS KNIGHTS, Howard Pyle. Finest children's version of life of King Arthur. 48 illustrations by Pyle. 131pp. 6⅛ x 9¼. 21445-1 Pa. $4.95

CARUSO'S CARICATURES, Enrico Caruso. Great tenor's remarkable caricatures of self, fellow musicians, composers, others. Toscanini, Puccini, Farrar, etc. Impish, cutting, insightful. 473 illustrations. Preface by M. Sisca. 217pp. 8⅜ x 11¼. 23528-9 Pa. $6.95

PERSONAL NARRATIVE OF A PILGRIMAGE TO ALMADINAH AND MECCAH, Richard Burton. Great travel classic by remarkably colorful personality. Burton, disguised as a Moroccan, visited sacred shrines of Islam, narrowly escaping death. Wonderful observations of Islamic life, customs, personalities. 47 illustrations. Total of 959pp. 5⅜ x 8½.
21217-3, 21218-1 Pa., Two-vol. set $12.00

INCIDENTS OF TRAVEL IN YUCATAN, John L. Stephens. Classic (1843) exploration of jungles of Yucatan, looking for evidences of Maya civilization. Travel adventures, Mexican and Indian culture, etc. Total of 669pp. 5⅜ x 8½. 20926-1, 20927-X Pa., Two-vol. set $7.90

AMERICAN LITERARY AUTOGRAPHS FROM WASHINGTON IRVING TO HENRY JAMES, Herbert Cahoon, et al. Letters, poems, manuscripts of Hawthorne, Thoreau, Twain, Alcott, Whitman, 67 other prominent American authors. Reproductions, full transcripts and commentary. Plus checklist of all American Literary Autographs in The Pierpont Morgan Library. Printed on exceptionally high-quality paper. 136 illustrations. 212pp. 9⅛ x 12¼. 23548-3 Pa. $12.50

AN AUTOBIOGRAPHY, Margaret Sanger. Exciting personal account of hard-fought battle for woman's right to birth control, against prejudice, church, law. Foremost feminist document. 504pp. 5⅜ x 8½.
20470-7 Pa. $5.50

MY BONDAGE AND MY FREEDOM, Frederick Douglass. Born as a slave, Douglass became outspoken force in antislavery movement. The best of Douglass's autobiographies. Graphic description of slave life. Introduction by P. Foner. 464pp. 5⅜ x 8½. 22457-0 Pa. $5.50

LIVING MY LIFE, Emma Goldman. Candid, no holds barred account by foremost American anarchist: her own life, anarchist movement, famous contemporaries, ideas and their impact. Struggles and confrontations in America, plus deportation to U.S.S.R. Shocking inside account of persecution of anarchists under Lenin. 13 plates. Total of 944pp. 5⅜ x 8½.
22543-7, 22544-5 Pa., Two-vol. set $12.00

LETTERS AND NOTES ON THE MANNERS, CUSTOMS AND CONDITIONS OF THE NORTH AMERICAN INDIANS, George Catlin. Classic account of life among Plains Indians: ceremonies, hunt, warfare, etc. Dover edition reproduces for first time all original paintings. 312 plates. 572pp. of text. 6⅛ x 9¼. 22118-0, 22119-9 Pa.. Two-vol. set $12.00

THE MAYA AND THEIR NEIGHBORS, edited by Clarence L. Hay, others. Synoptic view of Maya civilization in broadest sense, together with Northern, Southern neighbors. Integrates much background, valuable detail not elsewhere. Prepared by greatest scholars: Kroeber, Morley, Thompson, Spinden, Vaillant, many others. Sometimes called Tozzer Memorial Volume. 60 illustrations, linguistic map. 634pp. 5⅜ x 8½.
23510-6 Pa. $10.00

HANDBOOK OF THE INDIANS OF CALIFORNIA, A. L. Kroeber. Foremost American anthropologist offers complete ethnographic study of each group. Monumental classic. 459 illustrations, maps. 995pp. 5⅜ x 8½.
23368-5 Pa. $13.00

SHAKTI AND SHAKTA, Arthur Avalon. First book to give clear, cohesive analysis of Shakta doctrine, Shakta ritual and Kundalini Shakti (yoga). Important work by one of world's foremost students of Shaktic and Tantric thought. 732pp. 5⅜ x 8½. (Available in U.S. only)
23645-5 Pa. $7.95

AN INTRODUCTION TO THE STUDY OF THE MAYA HIEROGLYPHS, Syvanus Griswold Morley. Classic study by one of the truly great figures in hieroglyph research. Still the best introduction for the student for reading Maya hieroglyphs. New introduction by J. Eric S. Thompson. 117 illustrations. 284pp. 5⅜ x 8½. 23108-9 Pa. $4.00

A STUDY OF MAYA ART, Herbert J. Spinden. Landmark classic interprets Maya symbolism, estimates styles, covers ceramics, architecture, murals, stone carvings as artforms. Still a basic book in area. New introduction by J. Eric Thompson. Over 750 illustrations. 341pp. 8⅜ x 11¼.
21235-1 Pa. $6.95

GEOMETRY, RELATIVITY AND THE FOURTH DIMENSION, Rudolf Rucker. Exposition of fourth dimension, means of visualization, concepts of relativity as Flatland characters continue adventures. Popular, easily followed yet accurate, profound. 141 illustrations. 133pp. 5⅜ x 8½.
23400-2 Pa. $2.75

THE ORIGIN OF LIFE, A. I. Oparin. Modern classic in biochemistry, the first rigorous examination of possible evolution of life from nitrocarbon compounds. Non-technical, easily followed. Total of 295pp. 5⅜ x 8½.
60213-3 Pa. $4.00

PLANETS, STARS AND GALAXIES, A. E. Fanning. Comprehensive introductory survey: the sun, solar system, stars, galaxies, universe, cosmology; quasars, radio stars, etc. 24pp. of photographs. 189pp. 5⅜ x 8½. (Available in U.S. only)
21680-2 Pa. $3.75

THE THIRTEEN BOOKS OF EUCLID'S ELEMENTS, translated with introduction and commentary by Sir Thomas L. Heath. Definitive edition. Textual and linguistic notes, mathematical analysis, 2500 years of critical commentary. Do not confuse with abridged school editions. Total of 1414pp. 5⅜ x 8½.   60088-2, 60089-0, 60090-4 Pa., Three-vol. set $18.50

Prices subject to change without notice.

Available at your book dealer or write for free catalogue to Dept. GI, Dover Publications, Inc., 180 Varick St., N.Y., N.Y. 10014. Dover publishes more than 175 books each year on science, elementary and advanced mathematics, biology, music, art, literary history, social sciences and other areas.